No Shy Colleen

*Stories of
Irish American Women
in the United States
in the 19th and
Early 20th Centuries*

Written by Pat Commins
and Elizabeth Rice

Chapbook Press

Schuler Books
2660 28th Street SE
Grand Rapids, MI 49512
(616) 942-7330
www.schulerbooks.com

No Shy Colleen: Stories of Irish American Women in the 19th and Early 20th Centuries

ISBN 13: 9781966196365

Library of Congress Control Number: 2025921784

Cover design by Krystal Birchmeier at American Speedy Printing

Back cover illustration courtesy of Tricksy Wizard Comics

Printed in the United States by Chapbook Press.

To all of the women who made the journey and all who endured.

For Harrison, William, Charles, Theodore and Juliette:
You are the brightness of our days.

Contents

Acknowledgments

With thanks to the librarians, archivists, local historians and members of historical societies who answered our queries and encouraged our efforts. Special thanks to David Gutierrez and Rose Rice for assistance with photos and to Cathy Rice for assistance in research. Thanks to tricksywizard.com Trout and Adam for drawings. We especially thank our families for their support during this endeavor. WBSFA

Introduction

No Shy Colleen

SHY—adjective; being reserved or having or showing nervousness or timidity in the company of other people; from the Old English 'sceoh' (of a horse) easily frightened

Oxford Languages Dictionary

COLLEEN—noun; an Irish term for a girl or young woman; from the Irish Gaelic 'caile' countrywoman early-19th century

Oxford Languages Dictionary

The idea for this collection of stories grew from something we learned while researching stories for our first book, "Irish Immigrants in Michigan: A History in Stories". That book contained one story about Irish immigrants in the 19th century from each of Michigan's 83 counties. In spite of the large number of Irish immigrants who settled in Michigan during this time, there were very few recorded stories about Irish immigrant women. Where were the women's stories? They were not in the published compilation books of the time that detailed the lives of prominent men who became important industrialists or politicians or religious leaders or dignitaries. Once the Michigan book was completed, we decided to research the lives of Irish immigrant women in the United States in the 19th and early 20th centuries. Again, it was a challenge to find women's stories but we persevered. The stories of the courage, compassion and determination of these Irish women to make new lives in America are as important as all immigrant, indigenous and pioneer stories because they are a part of American history as it unfolded during this time even if they were not recorded.

In the 19th century, Ireland was part of the British empire. Most of the people in Ireland were very poor tenant farmers because the English government had given thousands of acres of land to Englishmen who were loyal to England during Cromwellian campaigns against Ireland in the 17th century. This resulted in 97% of the land in Ireland belonging to mostly absent landlords. The landlords rented small parcels of land to

Irish families. The tenant farmers paid their rent by growing grain crops for the landlord and tending to his fields. They were allowed to grow potatoes for their families on a very small section of the rented land. The potato became the staple food for most of the people in Ireland.

The small house of the tenant farmer included the farmer, his wife and children and sometimes other relatives. The mother in the family managed the household chores and looked after young children. The mother and daughters undertook the spinning, weaving and sewing of clothing for the family. They churned butter, weeded the crop field, saved hay and dug the turf or peat used for fuel. Many women were able to sell excess butter or wool which brought in much needed income. In the early years of the 19th century, both women and men were often able to contribute equally to the financial welfare of the family.

The year 1845 was the beginning of An Gorta Mor, the Potato Famine in Ireland. The potatoes grown on the small, rented lots were infected with a fungus. The plants above ground withered while the potatoes underground rotted. There was no potato harvest that year. People managed the crisis by eating some of the stored seed potatoes they planned to plant the next year. The next year, the same thing happened again. The potato plants seemed to be growing well but then began to wither. When the people dug into the ground to check the potatoes, again, they were rotten. There were no seed potatoes to plant in the year of 1847. Thousands of people starved and died.

There was plenty of other food in Ireland during the famine years. The grain harvests and cattle were exported to England and beyond. When the people became too weak from lack of food, they could not plant the crops which paid their rent. Landlords began evicting people from their rented lots. The land was turned to grazing which was far more profitable. Homeless and starving now, people in Ireland began to think of immigration as their only hope for survival.

During the famine years, entire families sold all they had to procure tickets for passage on a ship heading to Canada or the United States. Sometimes, a family could afford to send only one member across the ocean. This was usually a son, but sometimes, it was a daughter who immigrated. The idea was for the emigrant to find work, save as much money as they could, then send money back home so that another family member could immigrate. The pattern continued until the family was reunited again. This chain migration was carried out over many years.

The potato crops recovered beginning around 1851. The people who had remained in Ireland were still living in dire poverty. Young women, especially, no longer had opportunities to contribute to their family's income. Those who had relatives in America, or who heard from friends in America, learned that there were opportunities for women to make a living in America. This led to more women immigrating on their own. Immigrating to America also allowed young women to envision a different sort of life than what was the norm for them in Ireland. In America, they would be able to have some independence from a social system that allowed only a few roles a woman could aspire to in her lifetime.

When industrialized processes for many types of work once done by hand came into practice, many of the new machines required employees who were attuned to details, had nimble and quick fingers and could stand repetitive work in less than ideal manufacturing spaces. Company owners believed that women were a good fit for these types of jobs. Additionally, immigrant women would work for low pay. The young Irish women who landed in New York City, Boston, Philadelphia and other East Coast cities became employees of these manufacturing firms. Others became domestic servants, toiling for the more affluent families in these cities. While the hours were long and the work exhausting, domestic servants usually lived in their employer's house. This saved the expense of paying for their room and board. By the end of the 19th century, Irish women immigrants to the United States outnumbered the Irish men immigrating.

The independence that these young Irish women came to regard as their right led many of them to imagine a future not bound by the prevailing societal conventions. More and more women left the East Coast cities for new lives in unsettled areas of the country. These women became pioneers, farmers, homesteaders, miners, traders, soldiers, teachers, nurses, doctors and women of business. Some of these women were married when they challenged societal barriers. Other women were single by choice or circumstance when they broke economic and social barriers. Single parent mothers raised their children, saw to their education and kept a roof over their family's heads while running their farms, ranches and businesses. Women in religious orders often found themselves in leadership roles generally reserved for men.

In general, people living in America in the 19th century had an understanding of what a morally upstanding woman should be like: how she should dress, act and speak. Many people thought that women were inferior to men in intellect, strength and business acumen. The conditions and situations that many women found themselves in as they created new lives in America called for them to be resilient, strong, brave, smart and practical. Often, decorum had to be sacrificed for a greater good. One lesson that Irish immigrant women learned was the importance of a good education. While many of the Irish women who immigrated to America did not know how to read or write, they were all determined that their children, both sons and daughters, would have these advantages and many more so that they could provide for themselves and their families just as their mothers had done for them.

These are the true stories of Irish immigrant women and/or their daughters born in America who made a difference, for the good, by the nature of the lives they lived. We have included one story from each of the fifty states and the District of Columbia. Most of these women received very little notice, if any, in the newspapers of the time, or in biographical books. It is time to tell their stories.

Discrepancies of names, places, dates and events may have occurred, as sources sometimes differed and primary sources were not always available or accessible.

"I was no shy colleen."

—*Eva Montgomery McGown: Alaska*

"Above all else, deep in my soul, I'm a tough Irish woman."

—*Mary Harris Mother Jones: West Virginia*

ALABAMA:

Planting the Seeds of Knowledge

Margaret Murray Washington

For many different reasons, in the 19th century, people did not always know about their immediate family history. Some people did not know with certainty the names of their own parents. Accurate information was not always written down. Dates may have been approximated and places of birth could be unknown. Family members were often separated from each

other. Many people could neither read nor write. Thousands of Irish immigrants coming into the United States during the 19th century did not speak or understand the English language, the language of official forms in the country. For many children, it was enough to know that they had a father and a mother. In safe environments, their lives could carry on with that much information.

Margaret Murray Washington was one such child born to parents about whom very little is known. Her mother may have been called Lucy, born in Georgia in the early 19th century. Lucy may have been an enslaved woman at some time. She may have later worked as a washerwoman. Her father was

"Mrs. Booker Washington" George Grantham Bain Collection Creator: Bain News Service ca. 1910- ca. 1915. Courtesy of Library of Congress Prints and Photographs Division LC-DIG-ggbain-20376

thought to be James Murray, an Irish immigrant who may have been born around the year 1820 in Ireland. It is not known when James immigrated to the United States. He came to live in Mississippi City, Mississippi. James may have worked as a sharecropper and also on a railroad crew.

There are two accounts of Margaret's birthdate, March 9, 1861 or March 9, 1865. She was born in Macon, Noxubee County, Mississippi. Margaret was one of a number of siblings. Her father James passed away when she was seven years old. Margaret was taken into care by a brother and sister who were practicing Quakers. She was encouraged by her foster care adults to pursue an education. Margaret excelled as a student. She was offered a teaching position when she finished school at the age of fourteen. Instead of accepting the teaching position, Margaret desired to continue her education at Fisk Preparatory School in Nashville, Tennessee.

Fisk College, eventually Fisk University, served a population of black and brown students. Margaret pursued a liberal arts education. When she graduated in 1889, she elected to stay on at Fisk as a teacher. The following year, she met Booker T. Washington, a former enslaved person who lived with his family in West Virginia after emancipation. He was an ardent believer in education, a teacher, a gifted speaker and an activist. He founded the Tuskegee Institute in Alabama offering higher education for black communities in Alabama. Mr. Washington offered Margaret the position of "Lady Principal". Margaret accepted the position which paid her a salary of $500 per year. She taught English classes and was the head of the Women Industries Department. Eventually, Margaret and Booker T. Washington married in 1892. Margaret had initially refused Booker's proposal of marriage because his children from two previous marriages were not welcoming to her.

As Mrs. Booker T. Washington, Margaret could have remained at home, busy with children and household affairs. She stayed on at the Tuskegee Institute, working with Booker to enlarge the school in order that more members of the black community could attend. Booker gave many presentations around the country promoting the school and the need for higher education for black students. Margaret assisted her husband in writing his speeches. She accompanied him often during his travels.

While Booker was giving his speeches, Margaret often spoke to the women who attended these presentations. She believed that black and brown women should have access to the kinds of classes taught at Fisk as well as programs that would benefit them in their daily lives. She inaugurated child care classes, provided child care workers-even herself at times. She held classes in literacy training, home care and hygiene. She called her meetings, 'mother's meetings'. Margaret organized the Tuskegee Woman's Club whose members were educated women. She beseeched these women to get to know the local black farming communities and the women living on farms. Many of these women lived far away from any opportunity to learn about best practices for managing a home and caring for children. Margaret believed in women helping women to overcome economic and social difficulties. Margaret said to the Woman's Club members, "We knew that as they were lifted up, so might we rise."

In July, 1895, Margaret traveled to Boston, Massachusetts where women were gathering to join the newly formed National Federation of Afro-American Women. Margaret was elected president of the organization in 1896. During her tenure, Margaret was instrumental in merging her organization with members of the Colored Women's League. The new organization was named the National Association of Colored Women. Margaret served as president of this organization for many years.

In 1899, Margaret and Booker were gifted with a trip to Europe by affluent people who supported their work. Margaret met Queen Victoria and also visited the Stanley Horticultural College. It was the latter visit that had far-reaching ramifications for Margaret and many of her students at Tuskegee. Before visiting the horticultural college, Margaret had been introduced to the idea of agricultural and horticultural pursuits as innovative viable options for young women students. Agricultural learning was a key foundation of the Tuskegee Institute. Students grew their own food, raised livestock, kept bees and worked the land. Women were still primarily encouraged to take up trades traditionally allowed to them: sewing, millinery, nursing and dressmaking. When she visited the Stanley Horticultural College, Margaret saw women engaged in many types of garden work, from sowing seeds to growing food to working in a laboratory learning about grafting plants. As well, these women were studying chemistry, botany and zoology.

Margaret was excited to inform her students back at Tuskegee that there were opportunities for earning a living in the horticultural world. She was also interested in seeing her students take the horticultural knowledge they gained back to their home communities. As soon as Margaret returned to the Institute, she set right to work developing and promoting the new curriculum in horticultural pursuits. The women students worked in the field, learning about groundskeeping, planning and planting ornamental and decorative gardens as well as managing a garden for nutritional needs. There were courses on designing roadways and parks as well. Beekeeping, pollination and the importance of birds in a garden were also taught. The course Margaret designed required two years of study. Margaret stressed that the women should carry their knowledge with them to share with other women.

Margaret cared for Booker's two sons, Booker Talliaferro, born in 1887 and Ernest, born in 1889. The family moved into a large house on three acres of land on the Tuskegee campus in 1901. The home was called 'The Oaks'. Well known politicians and philanthropists visited the Washingtons in their home. Margaret entertained faculty and staff in their home on Sunday afternoons. President Theodore Roosevelt visited the Washingtons here. When Booker was suffering from kidney failure in his later years, he insisted that he be brought back to The Oaks. He died there in 1915. After his death, Margaret carried on her activism. She founded schools and worked for prison reform, including the abolition of chain gangs and lynchings. She remained dedicated to empowering black and brown women. She continued to walk into the farm fields to find women so that she might talk with them while she worked alongside them.

On June 4, 1925, Margaret passed away at The Oaks. Messages of condolence came from across the country. President Calvin Coolidge extended his sympathies. Margaret was remembered as a woman who advocated for social reforms, equitable education, amicable relationships between people, civil rights for all, and a fair system of legal justice. She was known as a compassionate person and an inspirational leader. One of the Tuskegee Institute buildings bears her name in tribute to the woman who lifted up so many others. Margaret Murray Washington was inducted into the Alabama Women's Hall of Fame in 1972.

ALASKA:

"No Shy Colleen"

Eva Montgomery McGown

"Eva Montgomery McGown" Courtesy University of Alaska Fairbanks

Eva Montgomery McGown was born in the town of Belfast, County Antrim, Ireland on June 23, 1883. Her parents were Frederick and Jane Montgomery. Eva was raised in luxury and affluence. She once stated that she and her sisters "wore seven petticoats under our muslin frocks and carried silk parasols to shade our faces from the sun." It was expected that Eva would 'marry well' and live in a house where she was catered to by servants. She was an accomplished musician and a singer. She directed a choir in Belfast for many years.

When Eva was thirty-one years old, her life took a decidedly different turn than the plan laid out for her by her family. She met a man named Arthur McGown. Arthur was an educated man who had traveled widely. He and Eva became friends and then decided to marry. Arthur, however, was planning to leave soon for Fairbanks, Alaska. Fairbanks was nearly four thousand miles away from Belfast. Eva was determined to join Arthur, much to the surprise of her family. In later years, Eva said in an interview with the writer Dorothy Walworth, "My love was a grief to everyone at home. They could not understand how I could go to a place at the end of the world, all for a man ten years older than I. What made my mother weep most was the weary thought that I must make the whole journey alone."

Eva endured a rough ocean crossing, sailing from Belfast to New York. It then took her six days to cross the continental United States by train. When she reached Seattle, Washington, a friend of Arthur's met and guided her to a boat that would carry her to the port at Valdez, Alaska. She stepped onto the boat in February 1914 and made ready to cross the Gulf of Alaska. There were no other women on the boat. The boat became covered in ice but still managed to land safely in Valdez. The sight of mountains and snow and the frigid cold impressed upon Eva just how far away she was from her home in Ireland.

The next stage of Eva's journey was to get from Valdez to Fairbanks. This journey lasted more than one month. Eva traveled by horse and dogsled. She traveled in a caravan and was again the only woman in the group. Each night the caravan stopped in rustic roadhouses. Eva was given her own room. Neither the rough conditions nor the blizzards that besieged the group frightened Eva. Her traveling companions were kind and brought her hot bricks to keep her warm. Finally, the caravan reached Fairbanks! Eva and Arthur were married on the very day that she arrived in the town. Arthur had arranged a three room log cabin for their home. He was part owner of the Model Cafe in Fairbanks. This was a gathering place for miners hoping to strike it rich in gold.

Eva and Arthur had been married five years when Arthur became ill. Eventually, Arthur was no longer able to run the cafe nor even leave the cabin. Eva took care of Arthur for ten years until his death. She undertook all of the work around their home that Arthur used to do-cutting and stacking wood, keeping fires lit, drawing water and shoveling paths through the snow. Her physical strength increased along with her compassion for Arthur.

After Arthur's death, Eva was at a loss, from grief and because she had no income. Caring for Arthur had cut her off from the other people of Fairbanks. She knew it was time for her to begin again. Eva found some temporary work and also began volunteering her services in the local hospital. She began writing letters to women who had just relocated to Alaska. She knew they would be feeling cut off and lonely, far from the homes they had once known. Eva invited newcomers into her home. She made meals for them and let them ask questions about life in Alaska. Eventually, whenever a newcomer came into Fairbanks, someone in the town would say, "You ought to see Eva McGown."

When World War II was underway, hundreds of servicemen and civilians flooded into Fairbanks. There was an acute housing shortage. The city government of Fairbanks called upon Eva to be in charge of finding housing, or at least rooms, for all of these people. Eva was paid a salary for her work which became her calling. She found beds for anyone who needed a place to stay. When the war ended, many of the people who had been stationed in Fairbanks chose to stay. Hundreds more people arrived to work on the Alaska Highway. More housing was needed. Eva became the city's official hostess, working tirelessly for anyone who needed her assistance. She was officially designated 'the honorary hostess for all of Alaska' by the territorial governor in 1953. Throughout her life, it was reckoned that she assisted 50,000 people in finding housing and adjusting to life in Alaska.

Eva enjoyed music as well. She directed the choir of St. Mathew's Episcopal Church in Fairbanks as well as serving as the church organist. In 1971, a music room on the campus of the University of Alaska Fairbanks was dedicated to her and named for her. The president of the university, William R. Wood, informed the audience in attendance about Eva's long history of teaching music and directing choirs going all the way back to her life in Belfast. Eva was then invited to speak to the audience. She told them, "I was no shy Irish Colleen, not me." From her home in the Nordale Hotel in downtown Fairbanks, Eva continued to serve as a goodwill ambassador for the city of Fairbanks and all of Alaska. She traveled widely in her later years, even returning to Ireland. Her heart was in Alaska though so she was always happy to return.

In 1972, the Nordale Hotel caught fire. Four people were killed in the blaze. Eva McGown was one of the victims. She died on February 22, 1972 at the age of eighty-nine years. She is remembered today as a woman who served others with compassion and wit and merriment and determination. She helped thousands of people find a welcome and a home in Alaska.

ARIZONA:

The Angel of Tombstone

Ellen O'Kissane, Nellie Cashman

Ellen, 'Nellie' Cashman was born in, or near Midleton, County Cork, Ireland in August, 1845. Her parents were Patrick and Frances Cronin Cashman. Nellie had a sister, Mary Frances, known as Fannie, who was born in 1847. In 1850, while the Irish potato famine was ongoing, Frances Cashman decided that she and her two young daughters would immigrate to America. They arrived in Boston that same year. The family lived in Boston for several years. In the year 1865, Nellie was working as an elevator operator in a hotel. It was unusual for a woman to be hired for this work.

"Nellie Cashman 1844-1925" Alaska State Library Portrait File Alaska State Library-Historical Collections

One day, during Nellie's shift at the hotel, General Ulysses S. Grant, the military leader of the Union forces currently engaged in war with the Confederate forces, stepped inside. General Grant struck up a conversation with Nellie. Nellie impressed the general and so he told her, "Go West and find more opportunity for fortune." Nellie took his words to heart. A few years later, in 1869, the family left Boston for San Francisco. They went to the home of a man named Thomas Cunningham. Thomas had been a neighbor of theirs back in Ireland. He and the Cashmans had immigrated at the same time and traveled on the same ship.

Fannie and Thomas married. The first of their children was born in 1872. Nellie found work as a cook in a restaurant. She and her mother then opened their own establishment which served food and provided lodging. Nellie also opened a supply store. Every day Nellie saw men coming into the town eager to mine for gold and silver. Nellie and her mother 'caught' mining fever. Nellie made plans to move to a mining town in Nevada. She set her sights on Pioche, Nevada. She planned to open a hotel and restaurant in Pioche because miners looking for silver were heading there. Nellie also planned to do her own mining as well. Nellie's mother did not want Nellie to travel alone so she decided to accompany her. They saved as much of their earnings as they could, then set out for Pioche.

When they arrived in Pioche, they were told there was only one place for sale near the town. The site was Panacea Flats, a few miles south of Pioche. In spite of warnings that they would be in dangerous territory, Nellie and her mother bought the site. Nellie told one of the miners who was trying to warn them away, "God had brought them from Ireland on that horrid coffin ship, settled them in the Irish slums of Boston, and landed them in San Francisco. He would watch over them here too."

Nellie opened The Miner's Boarding House a few weeks later. She and her mother worked in the kitchen as well as the dining area. Nellie met many miners. She listened carefully to all that they said about claims and mines and the gold and silver they found. She stored the information in her head, knowing that she would be better prepared when she began prospecting. The boarding house and restaurant business prospered. Nellie and her mother did very well for themselves. Nellie decided to try her hand at panning for gold. On her first try, she found a gold nugget! Nellie carried the nugget to a priest in Pioche, donating it for the building of the first Catholic Church there. Nellie used her earnings from the boarding house to send money to tenant farmers back in Midleton, Ireland so they could buy back land they had lost during the famine years.

Even with prosperity in Pioche, Nellie kept her ears open to new mining opportunities. Only one year later, she heard that gold had been discovered in British Columbia, 1,600 miles away from Pioche. Nellie made plans to get herself there. Her mother was not keen to move so far away from the rest of the family. Nellie traveled with her mother back to San Francisco so that she could live with Nellie's sister and husband and their two children. From San Francisco, Nellie traveled to Victoria, British Columbia. She traveled with a group of two hundred miners all eager to discover gold. When the group passed through Victoria, Nellie met some of the Sisters of the Order of Saint Anne living there. They were collecting money to build a hospital. Nellie donated to this cause and encouraged the other miners to give generously as well.

Nellie set up her mining equipment on the shores of Dease Lake in northern British Columbia. She lived near this lake for nearly two years. During the winter of 1874-1875, when no gold panning was possible in the frigid temperatures, Nellie headed back to Victoria. She carried with her $547 in gold nuggets. Nellie gave this money to the Sisters of Saint Anne to help run the newly built hospital.

During the trip back to Victoria, Nellie had heard about a group of men stranded by blizzard conditions in a mining camp in the Cassiar Mountain Range. The men had no means for getting food or medical supplies. There were reports that the men were suffering from diseases like scurvy. Nellie knew some of these men. She was determined that they must be rescued. She hired six men to accompany her to the camp. They carried 1,500 pounds of supplies, including limes to combat the scurvy. The camp was nearly 800 miles away from Victoria.

Soldiers in the Canadian Army met the group during their journey. The soldiers strongly advised the group to turn back due to the extremely dangerous weather conditions. Nellie served the soldiers tea and in that time convinced them that the trapped miners must be rescued. The soldiers relented. Nellie and her group pressed onward. They dealt with extreme cold and fresh snow falls which made travel difficult for the sled dogs whose feet kept sinking into the deep snow. Eventually, the sleds were abandoned and the group hiked with the provisions for the remainder of the journey. Nellie said to the men, "We may die, but if we do not continue these miners will die."

After 77 days, Nellie and the men found the miners in the camp. There were 76 men still alive, all in need of medical attention. Nellie got right to work, feeding and nursing the men. All of the miners survived, thanks to Nellie and the other rescuers. When springtime came round again, the entire party was able to make their way back to Victoria. They were met with cheers upon their arrival. Newspaper reporters hastened to Victoria to write accounts of the rescue. Nellie became known as 'the Angel of the Cassiar'.

Fame did not contain Nellie in British Columbia. Only a few years later, in 1880, she heard about silver strikes in the Arizona Territory. Nellie set out for Tucson, Arizona. She arrived in Tucson, but did not settle there. Instead, she moved on to Tombstone, Arizona, a town with a population that grew from 100 settlers to 14,000 in only a few years. Nellie once again opened a restaurant and boarding house. The business prospered. Nellie often passed a collection hat among her customers. She was raising money for the Sisters of Saint Joseph who wanted to build a church in Tombstone. They wanted to have a school built as well.

In December of 1880, Nellie received word that her sister's husband had died unexpectedly at the age of 41 years. Nellie immediately sent for Fannie and her five children to come to Tombstone to live with her. From then on, Nellie provided for the family. Three years later, Fannie also passed away. Nellie became a second mother to her nephews and niece, raising them to adulthood. The children witnessed their Aunt Nellie giving money and food to miners who were downtrodden and alone. They watched her nurse the sick and injured. The children learned that Aunt Nellie was known as 'the Angel of Tombstone'.

Nellie was a devout Catholic. When she learned that five men were to be sentenced to death by hanging for the crimes they had committed, she was distraught. She visited the men and offered them spiritual advice. The hanging was to be a public spectacle with a grandstand built for audience viewing. Tickets were sold for the event. Nellie petitioned the sheriff to have the grandstand removed but he was not inclined to do so. In the early hours of the morning, on the day of the executions, Nellie and some hired men dismantled the grandstand and disposed of the timber. The executions took place later that day but without a crowd watching.

In the mid 1880s, the silver camps in Tombstone were shutting down. Nellie knew it was time for her to move on once again to find other mining ventures. She did not want her niece and nephews growing up in mining camps. She sent all of them to boarding schools back in California. For the next several years, Nellie moved among different camps, always looking for the next big strike. In 1898, Nellie was in the Yukon region of Alaska. She made her home in Dawson City where she opened yet another restaurant, The Demonico. It was difficult to get provisions in the area so prices for everything were very high. Nellie could not make a profit here as she often gave her money to miners without any funds or to the Sisters of Saint Anne in Dawson City who were operating the hospital there.

Nellie remained in Dawson City for seven years. Her niece and nephews were grown and carrying on their own lives. One of her nephews, Michael, was a banker in Bieber, Arizona. He kept in touch with Nellie, always giving her credit for raising himself and his siblings. Nellie was nearing 60 years but was still moving among mining camps looking for another strike. She kept on prospecting into her eighth decade. When she was 79 years old, she fell ill with pneumonia. Nellie returned to Victoria where the

Sisters of Saint Anne Hospital took her in to nurse her. Nellie passed away on January 4, 1925. She was buried in Ross Bay Cemetery in Victoria.

The inscription on Nellie Cashman's tombstone reads:

Nellie Cashman 1844-1925. Friend of the sick and the hungry and to all men. Heroic apostolate of service along the western and northern frontier miners. Miner's angel, 1872-1924. In Nevada. In the Cassiar. In Arizona. In the Yukon. In California. In Alaska. Born in Ireland. Died with the Sisters of Saint Anne at St. Joseph's Hospital, Victoria, B.C. January 4, 1925. Requiescat in pace.

ARKANSAS:

I Walk Among You

Sister Mary Teresa Farrell
and the Sisters of Mercy

"Mother Superior Mary Teresa Farrell of the Sisters of Mercy"
Sculptor: Spencer Schubert Creator: Carol M. Highsmith,
photographer Library of Congress Prints and Photographs
LC-DIG-highsm-64748

The Sisters of Mercy, an order of nuns who trace the origin of their community to Dublin, Ireland in the early 1830s, were known as 'the walking nuns'. In contrast to contemplative or cloistered orders, the Sisters of Mercy left their convent each day to be among the people of Dublin. They taught the children of the city how to read and write. They taught young women skills they could take into the workforce so that they would not be destitute in their adult lives. The founder of the order, Sister Catherine McCauley, organized Sisters of Mercy Houses in the towns of Carlow and Naas in Ireland as well. She lived to see many young women answer a call to service before she passed away in 1841.

One of these young women was Alicia Farrell. Alicia was born in 1820 or 1821 to Christopher and Marianne Farrell. The family lived in Osberstown in the parish of Naas, County Kildare, Ireland. Alicia's father and his brothers were prosperous merchants who dealt in groceries, hardware and iron mongering. Her parents believed that Alicia should receive an education. After finishing at the local school, Alicia entered the Convent of

Mercy in Naas in 1841. She made a formal profession of her vows to the order in 1843. It was then that she took on a new name, Sister Mary Teresa.

During this time, a Catholic priest named Father Andrew Byrne was in Little Rock, Arkansas. He had just been appointed bishop of the newly named Catholic diocese of Arkansas. The population in Little Rock was growing, but most of the pioneering families were miles from Little Rock and from each other. There were also indigenous tribes who had been on the land for generations. Bishop Byrne wanted to see the Catholic community around Little Rock grow. He believed the answer to more settlers lay in his Ireland homeland.

The potato famine years in Ireland had left its survivors landless and destitute. So Bishop Byrne traveled to Dublin, Ireland in search of people to immigrate to Arkansas. He also wanted to encourage Sisters of Mercy nuns to come to Arkansas in order to teach these immigrants in schools he hoped to have built. Bishop Byrne made his way to Baggot Street in Dublin where the Sisters of Mercy resided. There were no Sisters in Dublin to spare so the bishop went to the town of Naas and the Sisters of Mercy convent there.

In Naas, the bishop found that all of the Sisters were willing to immigrate to Arkansas. Four Sisters were chosen, as well as five postulants, women in training to become nuns. One of the Sisters who volunteered was Sister Mary Teresa Farrell. She was the Mother Superior of the Naas community even though she was very young. Sister Mary Teresa would be the leader of the immigrating Sisters. The other Sisters who followed her were Sister Agnes Green, Sister Mary deSales O'Keefe and Sister Mary Stanislaus Farrell, a first cousin to Sister Mary Teresa. One of the postulants accompanying the group was Sister Mary Teresa's own sister, Mary Farrell.

Preparations for the journey commenced immediately. The group traveled to Dublin and stayed with the Sisters at the Baggot Street convent. They made many copies by hand of Bible verses and sacred music, as well as the rules of their order. On November 30, 1850, the Sisters left Dublin and boarded the ship, the *John O'Toole*. There were nearly 300 passengers on this ship, most of whom were recruited by Bishop Byrne. The first week of the journey across the Atlantic Ocean was uneventful. The Sisters held classes for the children on board in the morning and for the adults in the afternoon. For most of the passengers, this was their first experience of formal education. At the beginning of the second week at sea, a strong wind arose which turned into a severe storm. The *John O'Toole* was blown off course. When the storm abated, the ship was 800 miles off course, sailing near the coast of Scotland. The ocean journey lasted nearly eight weeks. Finally, on January 23, 1851, the ship sailed into the port of New Orleans, Louisiana.

The Sisters rested for twelve days, staying in a convent run by Ursuline Sisters in New Orleans. On February 2, 1851, the group boarded a Mississippi River steamboat, the Potomac, which carried them to Little Rock, Arkansas. The Sisters arrived on February 6, 1851. Little Rock had a population of only about 2000 people at this time. There was no convent for the Sisters so Bishop Byrne gave his house to the Sisters. The next day, people in town saw the Sisters walking on the dusty streets, visiting the sick and announcing their intention to open a school. Within a few months, Bishop Byrne had purchased a house which became both a convent and a school. Thirty-five students were enrolled. Most of the students were not Catholics. Some people in the town did not approve of children being taught in a Catholic school. Most of the settlers were pleased though to have their children attending a school whose teachers were well educated women. The Sisters welcomed all children to their school. Attendance grew rapidly as newly arriving immigrants were adamant that their children should receive a good education.

Within a short time, it became necessary to procure a larger building to accommodate the increasing number of students. Bishop Byrne found another property to purchase. The new property became St. Mary's Academy in Little Rock. Two years later, in 1853, Bishop Byrne once again called upon the Sisters. This time, he was looking for volunteers to travel to Fort Smith, Arkansas to set up a school there. Fort Smith was nearly 160 miles west of Little Rock, on the western border with the Oklahoma Territory. Once again, Sister Mary Teresa, now Reverend Mother Mary Teresa, volunteered to make the journey in order to start another school. She left with Sister Mary de Sales O'Keefe and some of the novices. When the women reached Fort Smith, they opened St. Anne's Academy. Their school was open to the children of the settlers as well as the indigenous children of the Choctaw and Cherokee tribes living in the region. The Sisters also opened a secondary school for young women.

The increasing enrollments in the academies necessitated the need for more Sisters to teach the children. In 1856, Bishop Byrne requested Reverend Mother Mary Teresa and a companion to return to Ireland in search of more Sisters of Mercy who would immigrate to Arkansas. The Sisters were away for one year. Upon their return, five more Sisters accompanied them. The academy at Fort Smith flourished. Next, the Sisters opened a school in the town of Helena, Arkansas, on the banks of the Mississippi

River. This was St. Catherine's Academy which opened in 1859. Reverend Mother Mary Teresa made the journey here with three other Sisters.

When the U.S. Civil War began in 1861, the Sisters had to refocus their energies, away from teaching and into nursing. Their schools, especially in Fort Smith, were close to battle fronts. They kept the school children inside all day long in order to protect them. At Fort Smith, the Sisters "raised chickens and cows, planted gardens, and foraged for berries to feed the children." The school buildings became hospitals where the Sisters cared for wounded soldiers, both Union and Confederate. The Sisters were not trained nurses so they did what they could to comfort the men. They gave them food, dressed their wounds and sat by their bedsides. As the war entered its second, then third, then fourth year, the Sisters found their schools becoming more like orphanages as so many children had lost fathers and family members.

In 1865, Reverend Mother Mary Teresa sent two Sisters to Chicago and two more to Philadelphia to be trained in nursing. When the Sisters returned, along with an instructor in nursing, the Sisters established a nursing school in Arkansas. The Sisters of Mercy also established a hospital in Fort Smith.

There always was a need for more Sisters to carry on this work so Reverend Mother Mary Teresa continued to make trips back to Ireland to recruit more young women for her causes in education and health care. She was indomitable in spirit. It was said of her that "nothing was too challenging for her." Reverend Mother Mary Teresa continued her work until her death in 1892 at the age of seventy-five years. Her tireless efforts made education possible for countless children in Arkansas in the middle of the 19th century. She did not ever turn away a child from the schools she founded. In recognition of her lifelong commitment to the people of Arkansas, a statue of her was put up in Gateway Park in Fort Smith. The six foot statue of Mother Mary Teresa shows her stepping forward, a walking Sister until the end of her days.

CALIFORNIA:

Equal Pay for Equal Work

Kate Kennedy

In the late 19th century in the United States, women were beginning to be allowed to take up professions that were previously only in the realm of men's expectations. Nursing and teaching young children had long been considered worthy work for women, although not regarded as professional work. Once a woman married, she was generally removed from the paid workforce. One young woman, who had received the benefit of some education while growing up in Ireland, used that education to become a teacher after she immigrated to the United States. She settled in San Francisco, California.

Kate Kennedy was born in 1827 in the townland of Gaskintown, west of the town of Duleek in County Meath, Ireland. She was one of seven children born to Thomas and Eliza King Kennedy. Her family owned a farm. This made them much more prosperous than most of their neighbors who were tenant farmers. She was able to attend the local school and then was able to attend a convent school where she studied four languages in addition to the English language. She remained at the convent school until she reached the age of thirteen. Her father passed away in 1840 so Kate was needed at home. She took on the duty of educating her five sisters at home.

The Kennedy family did not escape destitution and starvation during the potato famine years. In 1849, Kate, along with one sister and her brother, left Ireland. They found passage on a ship heading for New York City. The siblings arrived safely. Their plan was to find work and then, when enough money was saved between them, send for their mother and sisters to join them. Kate and her sister found work in an embroidery establishment. Two years later, the three siblings had saved enough money to send for their mother and other sisters. The family was reunited in New York City.

In 1853, two of Kate's sisters headed west to California. Thousands of immigrants were heading west, lured by the discovery of gold in California. These sisters wrote letters to the rest of the family telling them of the many opportunities awaiting them in California. The rest of the family decided to move west as well. They all arrived in San Francisco in 1856. Kate's sister Alice was already working as a schoolteacher. Kate and her sister Lizzie took the teaching examination required for working in schools in San Francisco. They both passed the exam with excellent marks.

It was not difficult for Kate to find work in a school. She accepted a position in an elementary school located near San Francisco. The school administrators in the area soon took note of Kate's work. In 1867, they decided to relocate her and promote her to the position of principal of the North Cosmopolitan Grammar School in the city of San Francisco. There were not many female principals of schools at this time, except in the schools run by religious Sisters. The promotion was a testimony to Kate's work. When she learned that her salary would be equal to that of a primary school principal, and not the same as a male grammar school principal, Kate questioned the policy. It was explained to her that, being a woman, she should not expect to receive the same pay as a male principal.

"Kate Kennedy School"
Courtesy San Francisco History Center, San Francisco Public Library, SFUSD NEG-44

Kate was not satisfied with this explanation, nor with the status quo regarding female teacher's pay. She began to lobby the California State Legislature to codify equal pay for equal work among women and men. Kate organized petition drives and gave speeches supporting the change in the law. In 1874, her efforts were rewarded with the passage of a law requiring equal pay for equal work. The law read, in part, "females employed as teachers in the public schools of this State shall in all cases receive equal compensation as allowed male teachers." The legal precedent came to the attention of suffragettes Elizabeth Cady Stanton and Susan B. Anthony. The women visited Kate in order to thank her for her efforts on behalf of women.

In 1886, Kate decided to run for the office of State School Superintendent. This was the first time in California state history that a woman ran for public office. She did not garner enough votes to secure the office, but she did set a precedent for women aspiring to influential and powerful positions of elected authority.

The following year, when Kate was sixty years old, her health began to fail. She took a two month leave of absence from her job in order to regain her strength. When she returned to work, Kate learned that the Board of Education had transferred her to another school and reduced her salary from $175 per month to $100 per month. Kate decided to fight this decision.

Kate initiated a lawsuit against the City of San Francisco. She was not seeking a monetary settlement but she did want to be reinstated as the principal of North Cosmopolitan School, with the backpay that was due to her. The case went on for three years. Finally, the California State Supreme Court ruled in Kate's favor. Her success set another precedent, that of tenure for teachers in public schools. It was now illegal for a teacher to be fired or demoted without just cause. Just cause was described as incompetence or misconduct.

Kate savored her victory but only for a short time. She passed away a few weeks later, on March 19, 1890. Her legacy lives on in the advances she facilitated for women in general, and for those in the teaching profession. She was an early supporter of labor unions and workers' rights. Her conviction that workers in all professions must be afforded the same respect as those that employ them makes her efforts as important today as they were over one hundred years ago.

COLORADO:
The Woman Behind the Man

Catherine Theresa Smith Mullen

"Catherine Theresa Smith Mullen"
Courtesy Denver County Public Library

The saying, 'Behind every good man is a woman' was the case for many of the prominent men whose names adorn historic buildings and fill history books. One such man who rose to prominence in the flour milling industry in Denver, Colorado in the latter years of the 19th century and the early decades of the 20th century was John Kernan Mullen. J.K. Mullen's rags to riches story was the realization of the 'American Dream'. He was an Irish immigrant who through hard work, ingenuity, compassion and practical business sense realized personal wealth beyond most of his contemporaries.

The story of J.K. Mullen's wife, Catherine Theresa Smith was not noted in newspaper accounts of her husband's successful business enterprise. To those who knew her, Catherine was esteemed. She was a charitable, stalwart and upstanding person in her own right.

Catherine Theresa Smith was born in County Cavan, Ireland in October 1850. Her widowed mother, Ellen Smith, three brothers and one sister were barely surviving during the years of An Gorta Mor, the Great Hunger. Ellen managed to keep her family together and somehow secured enough money for them to make the voyage to America. The Smiths immigrated to the United States in 1854. They landed in New Orleans, Louisiana. From New Orleans, they made their way to Iowa. They lived in Iowa for a few years. Catherine's three brothers established a freighting business in St. Joseph, Missouri. The family then relocated to Atchison, Kansas in 1863. The Smith brothers carted goods from Atchison to Denver. In Denver, the goods were delivered to mining camps. One day, while the brothers were preparing another shipment for Denver, they invited Catherine to ride along with them. It was summertime so the trip would not be too difficult. Catherine accepted their invitation. The siblings traveled over miles of plains until they came within sight of the Rocky Mountains. Catherine was amazed at the views of the mountains. She felt drawn to this new landscape. When she returned home to her mother, Catherine described all that she had seen. She convinced her mother into making the same trip so that she could see the mighty mountains. Catherine hoped to convince her mother to relocate the family to Colorado.

Catherine made two more trips with her brothers to Denver and the mining camps. One such trip took place during the wintertime when the air was freezing and the going was rough. The harsh conditions did not deter Catherine from her plan to move to Colorado. Sometime after this, the entire family did migrate west. They first settled in Nevadaville. Then, they settled in Black Hawk. Finally, they came to Central City, Colorado. Central City was one of the first mining towns built after gold was discovered nearby in 1859. During the gold rush, Central City was known as 'the richest square mile on Earth'. By the time Catherine and her family came to Central City, Main Street was lined with houses and store fronts. The larger frame houses were located near the town center. Smaller log houses made from yellow pine trees were being built as quickly as the trees could be felled. Horace Greeley, who came through Central City in 1864 noted, "of these pines, log cabins are constructed with extreme facility, and probably one hundred are now being built, while three or four hundred are in immediate contemplation."

In 1872, Catherine moved to the city of Denver. Her Catholic faith had always been important to her. She attended St. Mary Catholic Church and taught Sunday School classes there. One of the other Sunday School teachers was J.K. Mullen. He and Catherine met and became friends. Two years later, they married on October 12, 1874 in St. Patrick's Catholic Church in Denver. Catherine settled into married life and keeping house. J.K. Mullen set about going into business for himself. Ever since he had emigrated from Ireland with his family to New York in 1856, he had been working in flour mills. He was fourteen years old when he first started working in the mills. He worked his way across the country, eventually settling in Denver where he was hired by Mr. Davis of the Shackleton and Davis Mill. J.K worked his way up to the position of head miller. By the year 1875, he believed he had learned all that he could about the milling of flour. He was ready to own his own flour mill.

Catherine had money of her own that she had saved. She had access to investment capital through her brothers' freighting business. Her sister's husband owned some mining interests which were also available to Catherine for investment purposes. She owned some properties and she had stock in a loan association. Catherine actively took part in the business side of her family's enterprises. Her family considered her to be an astute businesswoman. J.K used his own and Catherine's money to go into partnership with a man named Theodore Seth. They leased the Star Flour Mill in North Denver from a man named John Smith. The Star Flour Mill was the oldest mill in the city. One year later, J.K bought out Theodore Seth's share of the mill. He renamed the mill J.K. Mullen and Company.

From the start, J.K proved to be both industrious and a practical businessman. The mill prospered. J.K went on to buy more flour mills and to employ more workers. He patented a procedure for milling flour which he then called Hungarian High Altitude milled flour. This flour became very popular due to its purity. The flour was sought after throughout the country. The J.K. Mullen Company saw their profits soar.

Meanwhile, Catherine was at home, welcoming her first child. Ella Theresa Mullen was born in 1875. She was followed by May Rose, Katherine Smith, Frances Edith and Anne. Anne Mullen lived only four years. There were also many relatives living in Catherine and J.K's home. Catherine's mother and J.K's father lived with the family. J.K's other family members migrated from New York City to live in Denver with the Mullens as well. Nieces and nephews who emigrated from Ireland also came to stay. Catherine kept everyone fed and nurtured. J.K usually left for the flour mills before 7:00 A.M. Catherine had a hot breakfast ready for him. She kept his supper warm in the oven even though J.K did not usually return home before 9:00 P.M. The family was faithful in their Sunday Mass attendance. They supported charitable causes. An account of J.K's success included some words about Catherine. "Mrs. Mullen proved to be a wonderful homemaker and companion for her husband...She was not a driving force but her influence was inspirational. She was never overindulgent in social affairs. Her home, her family, and her church filled her life. Her true worth was reflected in the inspiration her life contributed to the members of her family and to others about her." J.K himself often said, "that his success in business was largely the result of home influences."

By the early years of the 20th century, there were Mullen flour mills in several states and 1000 employees of the Mullen Flour and Elevator Company. J.K convinced other mill owners to consolidate with him, thus forming a network of mills and elevators. All of the employees participated in profit sharing with the company. There were not any strikes or difficult labor relations within the company. J.K and Catherine donated large sums of money to worthy causes they supported.

In 1915, the Mullens donated 15 acres of land for the building of a home for indigent aged persons. When construction was completed, the home had room for 200 people who would live there without cost and in dignity. The home was run by the Little Sisters of the Poor. The organization remained at the helm for 100 years. In 1924, the Mullens donated $750,000 for the construction of a library in the Catholic University in Washington, D.C. They also had plans to build a home and school for orphaned boys. They donated $40,000 for the building of a church in the town of Oriskany Falls, New York. J.K had first settled in Oriskany after his immigration to America. They donated thousands of dollars to hasten the building completion of a cathedral in Denver. In 1924, the John K and Catherine T. Mullen Benevolent Corporation was formed. Catherine and J.K wanted their philanthropic endeavors to continue after they had passed away. Catherine then donated one of the family's former homes, along with $70,000 so that a church would be built to serve the growing Hispanic community of Denver.

Catherine passed away suddenly in her home on March 23, 1925. She had been in ill health for several months previously, but her physicians believed that her health had been improving. J.K and three of her daughters were with Catherine when she died. She was seventy-four years old. In many ways, Catherine lived a quiet life in the shadow of her well known industry leader husband. Yet, by her husband's own admission, he was only able to be the industry leader and philanthropist that he became known for because of Catherine's influence in his life. Catherine may have stood, mostly unnoticed, behind J.K, but she was not quiet after all.

CONNECTICUT:

The Diary of a Domestic Servant

Mary McKeon Driscoll

Thousands of young women emigrated from Ireland to the United States in the 19th century on their own. Janet Nolan, author of "Ourselves Alone", reported that almost 700,000 young, usually unmarried women, traveling alone, composed most of the immigrants leaving Ireland between 1885-1920. In the years after the 1845-1850 potato famine, young women especially had a difficult time. Families were still very poor. By marrying at a young age, women could remove themselves from their families, thus lessening by one mouth, the daily struggle for families to find food. If marriage was not an option, a young woman would try to find a paid position. There were not many work opportunities for Irish women in rural areas. The only option that remained was immigration. Finding work in America meant that the young woman could send money home to her family.

Mary McKeon was born in 1867 in Keshcarrigan, County Leitrim, Ireland. Her family lived in the village of Tooman. Mary was the firstborn child of the seven children in her family. She had four younger brothers and two sisters. When Mary was thirteen years old, she emigrated from Ireland by herself. Once across the Atlantic Ocean, she made her way to the home of her aunt and uncle who lived in Hamden, Connecticut. In May of 1881, Mary found work as a domestic servant in the home of the Smythe family in New Haven, Connecticut.

Although Mary was only thirteen, she was not too young to be hired as a domestic servant. The benefits of obtaining such a position were immediate. Female domestic workers usually lived with the family that employed them. This meant that Mary did not have to find her own lodgings, nor pay rent for an accommodation. Her meals were included with the position. Mary stayed with the Smythe family for one and a half years, until November 1882. She was paid $133 during her tenure with the Smythe. This was a higher wage than she could have earned working in one of the textile mills or a factory.

Mary kept a detailed diary during some of her working years. She listed her daily activities and her daily duties. She described her employers' activities as well as her own leisure time activities. She wrote about her loneliness stemming from being so far away from her own family back in Ireland. She wrote about making new friends and visiting new places. In addition to writing in her diary, Mary wrote letters to her family in Keshcarrigan. She enclosed money in the letters. She hoped that the money could be saved so that other family members could join her in America.

After leaving her post with the Smythes, Mary's next job was with the Killam family who had a winter home on Money Island in the town of Branford, Connecticut. Mr. Killam was a coach maker. Mary was treated very kindly by her employers which was not always the case for Irish domestic workers. She was included in family gatherings and outings. Along with the daily cooking, cleaning, laundry and ironing, Mary went ashore most days to collect the post. She enjoyed the outings with the family. In the evenings when Mary was sewing or writing letters in the sitting room, Mrs. Killam read aloud to her children and Mary. Mary lived with the Killams from January 1883-March 1883.

On March 6, 1883, Mary changed employment again. She next worked for the Osborn family. The Osborns lived near the town center in New Haven, Connecticut. John and Charlotte Osborn had five children living at home when Mary joined the household staff. She was glad to be living in town once again. She had been isolated from social gatherings while living on Money Island. Her free time was usually spent writing letters to her family, especially her father. She kept a record of all those she wrote to, how many times she had written and the cost of postage for each letter. Between April and July 1882, while she was with the Smythe family, she wrote 89 letters, each of them costing between five to ten cents to post.

Mary had more duties in the Osborn household. It fell to her to "sweep, iron, do the laundry, wash the woodwork, fetch water from the barn, run errands and clean silver." When the Osborns entertained guests,

Mary saw to the guests' comforts. She was not the only domestic servant in the house so the work was divided among the staff.

Mary did not send all of her earnings back to her family. She kept some money for herself to purchase items she wanted. Even in this, she kept a record of the money she spent. "I went down town this afternoon and bought me some gloves 55 cent and the Diary in the New York St." She also attended Sunday Mass at St. Mary's Church in New Haven where she always put some coins in the collection basket.

Mary met other young female domestic workers. Some became friends of hers. They would attend church functions and church sponsored dances and fetes. The local priests kept a close eye on these events. They were, in part, occasions for young people to meet and mingle under close supervision. Mary met a man named Daniel Driscoll. Dan was the son of Irish immigrants. He lived in New Haven. In 1889, Mary and Dan married. Mary was twenty-two years old. They made their home in Branford, Connecticut. During their married years, Mary gave birth to nine children, five sons and four daughters.

After Mary was married, she no longer worked as a domestic servant. A woman's focus was meant to be the family home, her husband and her children. All of Mary and Dan's children received an education. The eldest son went to school through the 8th grade, while the youngest son was able to attend and graduate from college. None of the daughters went into domestic service. One daughter pursued a teaching career. Another daughter married and moved into her own home. Still another daughter worked as a clerk in a wire company. The youngest daughter found work as a stenographer for a firm.

In 1930, Mary's husband passed away. It was fortunate that the family already owned their home in Branford. The home was worth $4,000 at the time. Mary still had some of her children living with her. When Mary was a young person writing in her diary, she had already made her way alone from Ireland to America, found work, which though arduous, gave her an income and discretion over that income. She assisted in her brothers' emigrations from Ireland with the money she sent to them enclosed in her letters. When she left the paid workforce, she took on a different role which, while unpaid, provided her children with the foundation that allowed them to achieve all that Mary hoped for them. Mary McKeon Driscoll passed away on December 10, 1940.

DELAWARE:

The 'Bean a Ti' Woman of the House

Catherine Dougherty Gibbons

Thousands of Irish immigrants provided the labor that enabled the industries of the 19th century in the United States. The family at the head of one such industry, that of manufacturing gunpowder, hired mostly Irish workers for their powder mills. The du Pont Powder Mill Yards were originally located on the banks of Brandywine Creek near Wilmington, Delaware. Eleuthere Irene du Pont du Nemours emigrated from France with his father and brother after the French Revolution in 1799. They landed in New Jersey. Eleuthere was a chemist. His vision was to manufacture a better grade of ammunition than what was available in America. Eleuthere had assistance from Thomas Jefferson and some French investors to carry out his vision. Brandywine Creek was chosen because it had adequate amounts and force of water to operate all of the processes a powder mill would require. By 1802, Eleuthere had established his factory. From the beginning of construction, du Pont hired Irish workers. There were many people who were skeptical of the abilities of Irish workers, but Eleuthere was not one of them. In 1804, Eleuthere hired four Irish men as apprentices in the powder yard. A few years later, Eleuthere began assisting his employees who wished to bring their families over to America. Most of these immigrants became du Pont employees.

One of the du Pont employees was John Gibbons. John was born in 1821 in Cornwall, County Donegal, Ireland. John sailed to America in 1838. His first job at the powder mill was that of a laborer. He earned $15.50 per month. John met Catherine Dougherty when she was brought over with another group of du Pont assisted immigrants. Catherine was born around 1825. She was the daughter of Patrick and Margaret Dougherty, also of Donegal. Catherine and John married in 1846. The following year, John was chosen by Edward Hurst, a yard foreman, to learn all about the manufacturing of black powder. In that same year of 1847, the potato famine brought starvation and death to Ireland. The Irish du Pont employees and the du Pont family assisted over 1,000 Irish people to immigrate during this time.

Edward Hurst died in a powder yard explosion in 1863. John was chosen as the new powder yard foreman. He was given a significant increase in pay. He and Catherine had five children by this time. As the new Hagley Yard foreman, John was given a bigger house for his family. He and Catherine and the children moved into a three-story, six room stone house next door to the powder yard gates. While John was busy in the powder yard all day, Catherine was kept busy tending to their house and children. Like other women married to du Pont employees, Catherine had the opportunity to earn some money of her own by sewing and labeling powder bags. She could do this work in her own home. It was also common for women and children to peel willow bark which was used to make the charcoal needed for the powder.

"Catherine Dougherty Gibbons's Tablecloth"
Courtesy Hagley Museum and Library

With their rise in pay, Catherine began to add extra touches to the family home. She acquired lace curtains and lace tablecloths. She had a second-floor parlor which contained a matching set of walnut furnishings, including a dining table and a press, or hutch, for her linens. There were those who criticized Irish immigrant women who rose above their lower class status compared to their American middle class counterparts. Many of these Irish women moving into middle class status enjoyed having and displaying niceties around their homes. Lace curtains at the windows were one sign of an Irish family's increased affluence and status. It was reported that Catherine said, "I would rather have tea and a piece of bread on a linen tablecloth than I would a banquet on oilcloth." Lace and linen added to an Irish woman's identity as an American. As well, lace and linen were a sign of prosperity. These items were also produced back in Ireland by women so they formed a connection as well with their homeland.

Catherine and John believed in formal education for their children. Many of the children of du Pont employees attended the Brandywine Manufacturers Sunday School. The school was non-denominational and located on du Pont property. The school had begun in 1817 so that the children, both boys and girls, could learn reading, writing and sums. They were also given religious instruction. Children were not the only students in the school. Employees could also attend. For many, this was their first opportunity to receive formal education.

In 1873, John Gibbons was presented with a gold watch by the du Ponts in thanks for his many years with the company. Catherine kept the watch after John passed away in 1885 from pneumonia. She did not remain in their home after John's death. She moved to a house that she and John had bought in the Wilmington neighborhood of Forty Acres. At the time of John's death, he had over $5,000 plus real estate. Catherine was now an independently wealthy woman.

Catherine passed to her daughters the fine linens she had used in their family home. One of the tablecloths depicted a scene from the Last Supper of Jesus. 150 years later, the tablecloth, intact and delicate, came to Catherine's great granddaughter who donated it to the Hagley Library and Museum in Wilmington, Delaware.

Catherine Dougherty Gibbons made a new life for herself on the banks of the Brandywine River through the generosity of others and through her own determination. She left her impoverished life behind in Ireland. She blended the traditions she treasured with new ways of doing in America. Her family was of utmost importance to her, as was her faith. Along with a sizable legacy for her heirs, she also left her linen tablecloths and lace curtains, her connection with her Irish roots.

FLORIDA:

Changing Lives for the Better

Mary Brennan Karl

"Mary Brennan Karl" Courtesy Florida Commission on the Status of Women

Mary Muriel Brennan was born on November 2, 1893 in Harbor Beach, Michigan. Her parents were John and Mary Dee Cunningham Brennan. Mary's paternal grandparents, Robert and Mary O'Mara Brennan emigrated from Templeorum, County Kilkenny, Ireland in 1849. Initially, they settled in Whitehall, New York. John Brennan and his sister Mary were born in Whitehall. The family moved a number of times before coming to Michigan in 1867. They settled in Sand Beach which was later renamed Harbor Beach. John Brennan was a grocer and the postmaster in Sand Beach when he married Mary Cunningham in 1888. Besides Mary Muriel, there were three other children in the family.

The Brennan children grew up playing with their cousins who also lived in Sand Beach. These were the children of their Aunt Mary and Uncle John Murphy. One of the cousins, William Francis, or Frank, would grow up to be the governor of Michigan and a United States Supreme Court Justice. All of the Brennan children were well educated. They all also learned about civic responsibility, loyalty and the importance of hard work.

Mary Muriel Brennan graduated from the Noble School of Elocution in Detroit, Michigan. She also attended and graduated from Emerson College in Boston, Massachusetts. She was well known in Harbor Beach as a musical performer as well as an accomplished speaker. She often gave recitations in aid of charitable and fundraising causes.

In 1921, when Mary Muriel was twenty-seven years old, the family moved to Daytona Beach, Florida. Mary continued performing in community theater productions in Daytona Beach. In the same year, Mary Muriel married Frederick Karl. Fred was also from Harbor Beach. He and his father owned the local telephone company. Mary and Fred moved to their own home in Daytona Beach.

Mary took on a teaching position after her marriage. She began teaching business courses. In 1922, her daughter Kathryn was born. Two years later, a son, Frederick joined the family. The Karl family returned to Harbor Beach where they lived for a few years. A second son, John, was born but he developed pneumonia. Mary Muriel and Fred decided that their family would be better off in the warmer climate of Florida. They sold the telephone company and moved back to Daytona Beach.

In 1931, Mary Muriel began teaching business courses at the Opportunity School in Daytona Beach. This was a vocational school. During the years of the Great Depression, Mary Muriel expanded the curriculum to include courses in plumbing, welding, carpentry, electricity and automobile engine repair. She became the director of the school in 1937. She continued to increase the number of vocational classes for young people. When World War II began, Mary Muriel and her colleagues trained thousands of young people on different types of metal-working machines needed for manufacturing in the defense industries.

After the war ended the school became a training center for veterans, to assist them in retraining for civilian jobs in manufacturing. Mary Muriel wanted to expand the school even more. She met with two women, Mary McLeod Bethune and Eleanor Roosevelt to lobby for land from the federal government. The women procured the land and the school was expanded. The new name for the school became Daytona Beach Junior College. Eventually, one of the buildings was named the Mary Karl College of Workforce and Continuing Education. All of her life, Mary Muriel believed in the power of education to change lives for the better.

During the dedication of this new building, one of Mary Muriel's grandsons said about his grandmother, "Mary and her husband lost everything in the Depression, so she was not a person of wealth, but her passion is what carried this on. I think of my grandmother and Mary McLeod Bethune taking the train together to the White House to meet with Eleanor Roosevelt, who picked up the phone and called the Pentagon to get this rolling. This is a story of three women collaborating in the 1940s and how a single person, not of wealth, but with tenacity, set out to make this happen." Mary Muriel Brennan Karl passed away on August 8, 1948 at her parent's home in Daytona Beach after a short illness. The many lives she helped change for the better are her legacy.

GEORGIA:

A Mother's American Dream

Johanna Rath Kehoe

In 1850, while thousands were dying in Ireland, Daniel and Johanna Rath Kehoe, along with their seven children, boarded the ship *Brothers* and made the journey from County Wexford, Ireland to the United States. They came ashore in Savannah, Georgia on February 28, 1851. It was less expensive for the family to travel to Savannah than an East Coast city like New York City or Boston.

Johanna Rath was born in 1806. She was forty-four years old when the family left Ireland. Her eldest child was fifteen and the youngest was three years old. Johanna's parents farmed land near the parish of Monamolin, County Wexford. Daniel Kehoe was a tenant farmer working for Johanna's father. Johanna's father leased the land for his farm from the local landlord in the area. He leased eighteen acres of land. Of this, Dan leased one and half acres. It was on this one and half acres that Johanna kept house and raised her children. John was born in 1835. He was followed by Mary, Bridget and Anna, William, James and then Simon. The family had a fairly easy crossing over the ocean. When they reached Savannah, they, and the other immigrants, received a warm welcome. A reporter for the Savannah Daily Morning News wrote about the immigrant ship coming into the harbor. "It is rarely that we see a more respectable body of newcomers from any portion of Europe, than those brought by the *Brothers* and who we learn design settling in Savannah. May they realize their brightest anticipations, of prosperity and happiness in their new home."

The warm welcome helped to calm the surprise and discomfort the newly landed immigrants felt when they stepped ashore. They had been told, and had read in advertisements about life in Savannah, that they were coming to a pleasing climate facilitating good health. They were unused to the hot temperatures, the humidity and the mosquitoes. The swampy land was completely unlike their homeland. No one wanted to leave so the Kehoe family looked for a place to make their new home. They came to the Old Fort district of the city. This neighborhood in Ward 4 was home to many of the Irish immigrants in Savannah. The unskilled

Irish immigrant men mostly worked for the Georgia Central Railroad Company or on the docks along River Street. Some professionally trained Irish immigrants in the neighborhood worked in civil services. Many of the immigrants had also come from County Wexford so the Kehoe family felt some kinship with their neighbors. Many of the streets in Ward 4 were named for prominent men of County Wexford, Ireland.

Daniel Kehoe joined the other Irish men working as laborers. Three years after the family came to Savannah, an outbreak of yellow fever, malaria, spread throughout the city. Ward 4, crowded with cramped housing and suspect water systems, was rife with victims of the disease. Daniel Kehoe died from yellow fever in 1854. The family had no money to put up a headstone for him. He was buried in what was known as the pauper's field.

Johanna was now the head of the household. She had no means of earning money to support her children and herself. The older children all found jobs as quickly as they could. By pooling their meager earnings, the family was able to stay together. The youngest children were able to attend the local public school. Johanna had harbored hope that her children's lives would be free from poverty and oppression. It was this hope that convinced Daniel and herself that immigration was the only hope for their children.

"William Kehoe House" Courtesy of Georgia Historical Society, GHS 1376 Van Jones Martin, Savannah architecture photographs

One of Johanna's children, William, took a job after completing his education in the public school. He was hired as a molder in the Savannah Machine and Boiler Works when he was twenty-three years old. Casting and molding iron as an industry gained momentum in Savannah. By the time William was thirty-five years old, in 1877, he was the foreman of the Phoenix Foundry owned by James Monaghan. When James Monahan died in 1878, he left the foundry to his wife and William. Two years later, William bought out Mrs. Monahan's share of the foundry. He was now the sole proprietor. William changed the name of the foundry to Kehoe Ironworks. The company grew to become a leading employer in Savannah. William built a magnificent home and gave generously to charities. He became involved in politics, serving as the county commissioner for many years. He was on the board of many organizations. He owned a number of properties. William commissioned decorative ironworks to grace the city buildings and parks.

Johanna did not live to see William become wealthy and well known. She passed away in 1868 at the age of sixty-two years. William paid homage to his mother by remaining in the neighborhood of Ward 4. His mother's influence guided him to be generous during the years when his 'American Dream' was realized. For Johanna, hard times in Ireland had become hard times in America. She never stopped struggling to provide her children with a safe and loving home. Johanna's 'American Dream' was for her children to have better lives than she had ever known. In this, her dream came true.

HAWAII:

The Princess

Abigail Wahiika'ahu'ula Campbell

"Kawananakoa" PNLPC-12-07847
Courtesy Hawaii State Archives

Abigail Wahiika'ahu'ula Campbell was the daughter of James Campbell of Derry, County Londonderry and Abigail Kuaihelani Maipinepine Bright. Young Abigail was born in Honolulu, Hawaii on January 1, 1882. Long before Abigail was born, according to stories, her father James had lived through many adventures of his own, beginning when he left Londonderry, Ireland as a stowaway on a ship heading for Canada when he was thirteen years old.

The culmination of James's plan was not to settle in Canada, but to join his brother John, who had already emigrated from Ireland to New York City. The brothers did meet up again. James went to work for his brother as a carpenter. Their father, William Campbell, was a cabinet maker at home in Derry. He had trained his sons in working with wood. James worked with his brother for two years.

In 1841, James signed on as a carpenter on a whaling ship. The ship was heading for the South Pacific. He would be away for many months. Among the islands of the Tuamotus, a part of French Polynesia at the time, the ship was lost. James and two other crewmen were the only survivors. The men were able to float to one of the nearby islands. They were detained here for a number of years.

Nine years later, James was once again on board another whaling ship. The ship docked in the busy port of Lahaina on Maui in the Hawaiian Islands. James decided to remain in Lahaina which was the largest city on the islands at that time. He found work rolling barrels of molasses to ships in the port. James's carpentry skills were in demand on the Lahaina plantation where sugarcane was grown on a large scale. James met and married his first wife while he was working on the plantation. She was Hannah Barla and the daughter of a landowner. Hannah and James were together for eight years before she passed away. They did not have children. After Hannah's death, James inherited the Barla land. The windfall allowed James to form a company with two other men. Their company became the Pioneer Mill Company, a sugar processing plant which opened in 1860. The Pioneer Mill company grew to become the largest and most prosperous of the many sugar plantations on the Hawaiian Islands. During the U.S. Civil War, sugarcane grown in the Southern states was difficult to acquire. Sugar from Hawaii became a much sought after commodity. The price of sugar rose rapidly. Hawaiian plantation owners became very wealthy, though their laborers suffered from long, grueling hours in the fields. Often, cruel overseers used whips to keep the workers hard at their tasks. James used his riches to buy land on several of the Hawaiian Islands.

James married again in 1877. His second wife was Abigail Kuaihelani Maipinepine. James and Abigail welcomed two daughters into their family, Margaret and Abigail Wahiika'ahu'ula Campbell. Margaret died before she reached her second birthday. Six more children were born over the years, but only Abigail and three of her sisters lived to adulthood. Abigail graduated from the College of Notre Dame in California in 1900.

When Abigail was twenty years old, she married a member of Hawaiian royalty, Prince David La'amea Kahalepouli Kawananako. Their wedding took place on January 6, 1902. Even though the Hawaiian Islands had become a U.S. Territory in 1898, many Hawaiians remained loyal to the monarch. David was third in line to the Hawaiian throne if ever it was restored. Abigail and Prince David had three children, two daughters and one son. Prince David lived only another six years. He passed away at the age of forty in 1908 from pneumonia. Abigail's mother passed away during the same year. Her father James had died in 1900. James's accumulated wealth included millions of dollars and thousands of acres of land. All of this came to Abigail.

Prince David's brother, Prince Jonah Kushiro, ascended to his brother's place in the line of succession to the Hawaiian throne. The hope for a return to the monarchy had not dissipated. Prince Jonah died in 1922. Abigail Wahiiak'ahi'ula Campbell was now the next in line of succession. She bore the title of Princess of Hawaii.

Abigail became an advocate for the native Hawaiian people. Abigail did not share their hope for a return to the monarchy. Instead, she focused on promoting Hawaiian causes. She was the unofficial head of the Native Hawaiian community. She was the first woman in Hawaii to serve on the Hawaiian Republican National Committee. She became the party chair, serving for twelve years. Abigail registered to vote on February 8, 1922 after the 19th amendment of the United States Constitution passed. She became a role model for many. She demonstrated that women's voices should be heard in matters of policies affecting Hawaiian people.

Abigail's youngest child, Lydia, married a doctor named William Jeremiah Ellerbrock in 1925. They had one daughter who was given the name Abigail Kinoiki Kekaulike Kawananakoa, born on April 23, 1926. After Lydia and William divorced in 1927, Abigail was adopted as a Hanai child by her grandmother. Princess Abigail wanted her granddaughter to carry on the royal lineage in name. She wanted her to honor Hawaiian traditions and to support causes of the Hawaiian people. The legal adoption also entitled Abigail Kinoiki Kekaulike Kawananakoa to the largest share of her great grandfather's estate.

Princess Abigail Wahiika'ahu'ula Campbell passed away on April 12, 1945 in Honolulu, Hawaii. During her funeral, it was said of her, "Within her great and generous heart, within her amazing breadth of mentality, her infinite sympathy, her dauntless courage and her unshakeable constancy in the wise leadership of the people...lay her most significant patent of royalty..." She is buried in the Maura 'ala Royal mausoleum on the island of Hawaii. This daughter of an Irish immigrant loved the people of Hawaii and was beloved by them.

IDAHO:

The Role of the Mother

Mary Ann Chapman O'Farrell

"Mary Ann Chapman O'Farrell" Courtesy Idaho State Historical Society Idaho State Library

Mary Ann Chapman was born on March 31, 1840 in County Cork, Ireland. She immigrated to the United States with her parents during Ireland's potato famine of the 1840s. The family settled in New Orleans, Louisiana. When she was nine years old, in 1849, Mary Ann began attending the convent school run by the Ursuline Sisters. A few years later, in 1853, Mary Ann's father passed away. Mary Ann and her mother moved to Louisville, Kentucky where members of her mother's family owned a grocery store. Mary Ann helped out in the store. When she was fifteen years old, Mary Ann married John Lambert. They moved to Philadelphia, Pennsylvania. Their daughter Mary Ann was born in 1856.

Mary Ann and her daughter moved back to Louisville alone two years later. She returned to working in the family store. She met John Andrew O'Farrell, a gold prospector, when he came through Louisville. John and Mary Ann married in 1859. John adopted young Mary Ann. He had already made quite a name for himself as an explorer, soldier, pioneer and miner. John had been born in County Tyrone, Ireland in 1823. At the age of fifteen, he was one of a crew on a ship sailing for India. He served on other ships, one of which brought him to New York City when he was twenty years old. He served in the Mexican-American War and the Crimean War. After this, he turned to prospecting for gold, first in California and then in Colorado. John took Mary Ann and their daughter to Colorado where he continued prospecting. He struck gold in 1860.

Two events convinced John and Mary Ann to leave Colorado. The Homestead Act was passed into law in 1862. The Homestead Act opened up thousands of acres of land in the western United States to settlement. Next came the creation and official recognition of the Idaho Territory in 1863. John wanted to move to the Idaho Territory. The family joined a convoy of fourteen wagons, pulled by oxen and horses which traveled from Colorado to the Idaho Territory. The journey took four months. When the convoy reached the Boise Valley, John claimed land opposite Fort Boise which was located on the Oregon Trail. He began clearing the land and building a one room dirt floor cabin. The cabin was directly across from the main gate of the fort. This was the first log cabin built in Boise. Eventually, John owned twenty lots of land in the area.

Mary Ann was a devout Catholic. She missed having a church to attend. One day, not long after the cabin was built, she looked outside where she saw two men on horseback. Mary Ann signaled to John that he should invite the men inside. The men were Catholic priests. Mary Ann and John invited the priests to hold church services in their cabin. They hosted these church services for four years. After this, John donated land for a church to be built. St. Patrick's Church was then built. The church lasted only eighteen days before it was consumed by fire.

Meanwhile, more settlers were staking land claims and moving into the region. In 1865, Boise City was named the capital of the Idaho Territory. Three infantry companies and a cavalry company occupied Fort Boise for the protection of the growing resident population and for travelers on the Oregon Trail. Hostilities with the indigenous people also living on the land broke out at times. On one occasion, in 1867, soldiers pursued a leader of the Paiute Nation, Chief Winnemucca. They pursued him all the way to Oregon. He was charged with carrying out raids on settlers. More than 200 indigenous people were killed as well as 13 soldiers. More than 90 indigenous women and children were captured and brought to Fort Boise. The officer in charge of Fort Boise offered the children to any white settler who wanted them. The children were not allowed to be reunited with their own families.

The seven year old niece of Chief Winnamucca was adopted by John and Mary Ann. At her christening, she was given the name Rosa. Along with Rosa, six other children were adopted by the O'Farrells. Two years later, Mary Ann gave birth to a daughter Gertrude. Another daughter, Isabella, was born in 1870.

John was not yet done prospecting. He moved the family to Salt Lake City, Utah in 1871. The family lived there for seven years. John worked in the Ontario Silver Mine. Mary Ann gave birth to another daughter, Evelyn, in 1874. Teresa was born in 1876. Mary Ann raised all of the children alone while John was away in the mine or serving in the Utah Territorial Legislature. She suffered greatly when Isabella died at the age of seven years. Three more children died during the years that the family lived in Utah.

In 1878, the family returned to Boise. Two more daughters were born, Angela in 1882 and Regina in 1886. Mary Ann was known throughout the town as a kind, compassionate woman who was always ready to help anyone in need. Her adopted daughter Rosa died in the year 1890, the same year that Idaho was admitted into the Union as the 43rd state. Two years later, John built a large brick house to accommodate the large family. He and a partner invented and patented a more efficient type of coupling for train cars. The family's prosperity was assured. They were one of Boise's leading families.

On May 23, 1900, it was reported that Mary Ann O'Farrell had passed away the previous day. She had been in poor health for a number of months, yet still retained her good nature and vitality of spirit. With her five daughters and John gathered round her, she made her last wishes known to them. She gave the names of the pallbearers that she wanted to carry her casket. She asked that notes of thanks should be written to all of her friends who had sent flowers or messages to her during her illness. She said that her daughter Angela, soon to graduate as valedictorian from St. Teresa's Academy must do so and "think of her mother as if she were there." Mary Ann requested that the clock in her home should be stopped at the moment of her death. All of her wishes were carried out, even the hands of the clock, which were stopped at 12:28.

John and four of his daughters remained in the family home. The eldest daughter, Mary Ann, returned to her home and husband in Utah. John O'Farrell passed away five months after Mary Ann's death. The physician attending him said that John's grief over losing Mary Ann had hastened his own death. The O'Farrell daughters donated the first cabin that John built when they first came to Idaho to the Daughters of the American Revolution in 1910. The little cabin was considered the oldest house in Boise. The author of Mary Ann Chapman O'Farrell's obituary, did at the end of Mary Ann's life, find a way to give her recognition for all of her achievements. Her obituary states, "Mrs. O'Farrell was devoted to her home, her family and her friends, a kind mother, a loving wife and a pleasant companion."

ILLINOIS:

Civil War Soldier

Jenny Hodgers/Albert Cashier

"Albert Cashier" Gilder Lehman Collection
GLC07587 Public Domain

According to the American Battlefield Trust Organization, there are "over 400 documented cases of women disguising themselves as men and fighting as soldiers on both sides during the Civil War". One such person was Jennie Hodgers, an Irish immigrant born in Clogherhead, County Louth, Ireland. Wearing a disguise that made her appear to be a boy, Jennie stowed away on a ship heading for America. After safely arriving, she traveled west, settling in Belvedere, Illinois. Seeking employment as a man, Jennie found work as a farm hand and general laborer. When the Civil War began, Jennie Hodgers enlisted in the 95th Illinois Infantry on August 6, 1862. The name on the enlistment form read Albert Cashier.

Private Cashier served for three years as part of the Army of Tennessee. The Battlefield Trust records show that Cashier was present in more than forty battles. Among those were Vicksburg, the Battle of Nashville, the Red River Campaign and the Battles at Kennesaw Mountain and Jonesborough, Georgia.

Women were not permitted to be soldiers during the U.S. Civil War. Yet, Jennie Hodgers, as Albert Cashier, did enlist and was accepted by the other soldiers in the unit. Some of Albert's and others' reasons for enlisting were compiled by Deanne Blanton, co-author of the book, *They Fought Like Demons: Women Soldiers in the Civil War*. Patriotism and answering President Lincoln's call for soldiers persuaded some women to join. There was a compelling economic reason as well. A soldier's pay was at least twice as high as any wages a woman could earn working as a domestic servant or a laundress. Yet another reason, though one not traditionally associated with women of this time, was the excitement and adventure that many people believed wartime offered. Deanne Blanton went on to write, "The women who went to war, who disguised themselves as men and carried a gun, were overwhelmingly working-class women, immigrant women, poor women, urban women and yeoman farm girls."

After three years and after marching thousands of miles, Albert was mustered out with the remainder of his unit on August 17, 1865. He made his way back to Illinois and settled in the town of Saunemin, Illinois. He found work in various establishments and capacities, maintaining his identity as Albert Cashier. At different times, he was a farm laborer or a church and cemetery custodian or the town lamplighter. One benefit of Albert's status was that he could vote in all elections, a right not accorded to women until many years later. He collected his soldier's pension and had a bank account in his own name. Women who wished to have a bank account usually had to have their husband or father's name listed as the principal account holder.

Albert continued to live a quiet life in Saunemin until November 1910 when he was struck by an automobile. He was taken to the local hospital. Here, Albert's biological identity was discovered. The hospital staff honored Albert's wishes and did not make their findings known. Albert was sent from the hospital to the Soldiers and Sailors Home, located in Quincy, Illinois, for recuperation. He lived in the home for two and a half years. In March 1913, Albert was found to be suffering from a form of dementia. He could not remain in the Soldiers and Sailors Home anymore. He was sent to the Illinois State Hospital for the Insane. The staff members in the State Hospital would not honor Albert's wishes to be regarded as a man. He was forced to wear a dress. Newspaper reporters learned about Albert and wrote stories about the former Union soldier who was once known as Jennie Hodgers.

Albert's former comrades came to his defense. They held Albert in high esteem and rallied against his treatment at the hospital. Albert's former commanding officer spoke in his defense as well. A fellow soldier should not be denied his pension or his name.

Albert Cashier passed away on October 10, 1915. He was buried in his uniform. His tombstone bears his name, Albert Cashier. The inscription includes his military service details.

INDIANA:

Portrait of the Artist

Lucy M. Taggart

"Lucy M Taggart"(center) Courtesy Indiana Historical Society

One of the foremost painters of the early twentieth century was Lucy M. Taggart. She was born on March 7, 1880 in Indianapolis, Indiana to Thomas Taggart and Eva Dora Bryant Taggart. Lucy was the second child and second daughter of Thomas and Eva. Four other children were born between the years 1881-1888. Lucy's father, Thomas, emigrated from Emyvale, County Monaghan, Ireland in 1861 with his parents and some siblings. Thomas was five years old when the family sailed away from Ireland. 1861 was only a few years after the devastating Potato Famine. The worst of the starvation was over in Ireland but dire poverty was still the lot of many Irish people.

Thomas Taggart and his family settled in Xenia, Ohio. His father found work on the railroad. He was a baggage master. When Thomas was twelve years old, he went to work for the railroad at the depot restaurant and hotel as a cleaner. Thomas was a hard worker. He was promoted to working as a lunch counter attendant. He impressed his supervisors who transferred him to the Garrett, Indiana depot and then the Union Depot dining hall in Indianapolis. This dining hall was a well known gathering place for Democratic Party leaders and members. Visiting Democratic officials who arrived in the city by train made a beeline for the dining hall as well. Thomas overheard all of these people discussing politics. He became interested in political matters and public service.

In 1882, Thomas was promoted to the position of resident manager at the Union Depot. He and Eva had married in 1878 while he was working in Garrett. There were already three daughters in the family so the extra salary his promotion provided was added to the family's coffers. Thomas decided to step into the local political scene. He served as a precinct committee officer and a ward leader in Indianapolis. He was elected to the position of Marion County Auditor, serving from 1887-1895. This position was prestigious and paid very well. Thomas bought the Depot Hotel. Now he was meeting even more Democratic Party officials and becoming very well known in Indianapolis. He eventually purchased two more hotels in Indianapolis and the French Lick Springs Hotel in Orange County, Indiana. Thomas turned the French Lick Hotel into a world class spa which utilized the mineral-rich water from nearby artesian wells. The Taggart family's wealth and popularity rose with every year. In 1895, Thomas was elected the mayor of Indianapolis. He served as mayor for three terms, until 1901.

Lucy and her siblings grew up in wealth and comfort. Lucy was interested in painting and art from a very young age. She was encouraged to develop her artistic talent and her musical talent. She attended school at the Girls Classical School of May Wright Sewell in Indianapolis. After her graduation in 1898, Lucy planned to attend Smith College in Massachusetts. In the autumn of that year, Lucy left for college. She was only there for a few months when tragedy struck the Taggart family. Lucy's older sister, Florence, died while on a boat with friends near Bird Island, off the east coast of Louisiana in January 1899. An internal explosion destroyed the boat with all lives lost. Lucy came home from college to be with her family. She was now regarded as 'First Daughter' of the mayor, and as such, accompanied her father to various political and service functions.

Lucy decided to not return to college at Smith. Instead, she moved to New York City in late 1899. She wanted to continue her art studies and work on her own paintings. Lucy enrolled in the William Merritt Chase Art School. William Merritt Chase was a well known artist also from Indiana. Lucy also studied at the Art Students League of New York. She honed her skills as a portrait artist. After a few years, Lucy returned to Indianapolis in 1906 to enroll in the John Herron Art Institute. She studied under another Indiana artist, William Forsyth. She studied in Europe during a summer term in 1908. Back in New York City, Lucy met and became friends with Cecilia Beaux, another painter and Harriet W. Frishmuth, a sculptor. Lucy began to study sculpting. She developed her own style and her sculptures were highly praised.

From 1905-1929, Lucy exhibited and sold her work commercially. Her paintings, whether done in oils, pastels or watercolors drew attention and favorable reviews. The author of the book, "Art and Artists of Indiana", written by Mary Q. Burnet, published in 1921, wrote that Lucy's portraits were painted "with a subtle grace and a wealth of radiant color peculiarly rich in quality." Lucy belonged to the Society of Western Artists, a group formed to showcase artists from the midwestern region of the United States. She was also a member of the Pennsylvania Academy of Fine Arts in Philadelphia and the National Association of Women Painters and Sculptors.

In 1925, Lucy was among the artists chosen to exhibit selected pieces of their work in the inaugural Hoosier Salon exhibition which took place in Chicago, Illinois. The Hoosier Salon was the name chosen by the Daughters of Indiana, a group dedicated to highlighting the best of Indiana's artists. The Daughters of Indiana wanted the country and the world to know that artists from Indiana could and should be seen as accomplished and well known as artists from the East and West coasts of the country. Lucy exhibited two paintings, *Eleanor* and *Still Life*. *Eleanor* was awarded the Merit Award for figure composition. The following year, Lucy's entry, *Carnival* won the Merit Award for best picture painted by a woman artist. The Hoosier Salon brought more attention to Lucy's work and to herself as an artist. She continued to exhibit in the Hoosier Salon through 1931. In 1929, Lucy organized an exhibition in her father's famous French Lick Springs Hotel. For this event, thirty-eight sculptors exhibited their work. Lucy's good friend Harriet Frishmuth placed twelve of her own pieces in the exhibition.

After her father's death in 1929, Lucy's brother Thomas became very active in the Democratic Party. He served as a Democratic national committeeman during the 1930s. Lucy accompanied him to the Democratic national conventions of 1932 and 1936. She and Thomas met with President Franklin Roosevelt and his wife, Eleanor Roosevelt. They also met Vice President Harry Truman shortly before he became president after President Roosevelt's death. Lucy was invited to christen the U.S. naval ship, the *USS Indianapolis*. She broke a bottle of water from two of Indiana's rivers over the prow of the boat.

Lucy returned to live in Indianapolis to be near and help care for her mother. She accepted a teaching position at the John Herron Art Institute. Lucy taught painting classes and gave instruction in portrait painting but she did not accept any salary for her teaching. She donated some of her work to the institute and served on the arts committee. She did not marry, choosing instead to fill her days with family and friends. When her mother passed away in 1937, Lucy took on the role of head of her family. She did not sell her work commercially anymore but remained a vibrant member of the Indiana art world. As her own health began to fail in her eighth decade, Lucy sold the family home in downtown Indianapolis. Lucy passed away on October 9, 1960 in Indianapolis. She was buried in Crown Hill Cemetery next to her parents and other family members. She left an impressive amount of her work ensuring her legacy as one of Indiana's foremost artists of the early 20th century. Lucy Taggart's subtle grace and radiant color live on in her paintings and sculptures, much admired still today.

IOWA:
"Teach Without Seeming to Teach"

Sister Mary Frances Clarke and the Sisters of Charity

"Sister Mary Frances Clarke" Used with permission of Mount Carmel Archives of the Sisters of Charity of the Blessed Virgin Mary, Dubuque, Iowa

During a cholera outbreak in the city of Dublin in the early 1830s, five young women came together to dedicate themselves to relieving the suffering of those afflicted and to teach young girls to read and write so that they would someday teach their own children these skills. The women were Mary Frances Clarke, born to Cornelius and Mary Ann Quartermaster Clarke in 1802, Catherine Byrne, born in 1806 and soon after left at the Poor Clare Orphanage at Harold's Cross in Dublin, Margaret Mann, born in 1807 to John and Ann Thompson Mann, Elizabeth Kelly, born in 1809 to Michael and Mary Hyland Kelly and Rose O'Toole, born in Dublin at the same time. These five women were soon joined by a woman known as Mrs. Berkeley. She was the widow of a wealthy British army officer.

Mary Frances, Rose and Eliza all belonged to a Catholic sodality group. Eliza was friends with the daughters of Daniel O'Connell who was known in Ireland as the "Liberator" due to his efforts to secure Catholic Emancipation. Eliza traveled with the O'Connell sisters around Dublin serving the poor and ministering to the sick. The young women met Margaret Mann in 1831 when they came upon her sitting at the bedside of a suffering cholera victim.Catherine Byrne worked in the pharmacy at one of the Dublin hospitals. Mrs. Berkeley donated her wealth to buy food and medical supplies for Dublin's victims of cholera.

In December 1831, the group was able to secure a cottage outside of Dublin where they could meet. They would pray together and then decide upon their course of charitable works for the coming week. A few months later in March 1832, they secured a building and opened a school for young girls. The school was called Miss Clarke's School. It was located on Ann Street on Dublin's south side. Mary Frances wanted the pupils to learn to think for themselves. The women became known as 'the nuns of North Ann Street' even though they were not members of a religious order.

Eliza Kelly was the niece of the Reverend Mathias Kelly. Father Kelly gave his approval for Mass to be said in the chapel of the school building. A visiting priest from Philadelphia, Pennsylvania, Father Patrick Costello, was appointed the chaplain. Father Costello was visiting Dublin to share the plight of immigrant children in Philadelphia. He told the women that children were denied education. Instead, they endured daily grueling work in garment factories.

Father Costello's stories convinced four of the members of the group to immigrate to America where they would open a school in Philadelphia. On July 15, 1833, the women sailed from Dublin to Liverpool accompanied by the fathers of Margaret and Eliza. Before departing, a Mass was said for them by Reverend Peter Richard Kendrick. Unknown to the women at the time, they would meet Father Kendrick again ten years later.

The group sailed on the ship *Cassander*. They carried with them "five trunks, three boxes, six baskets and one bundle of wearing apparel." The women arrived safely in New York Harbor. Here, a crisis ensued. Eliza was carrying all of the money the women had brought with them to America. As she was descending the ship's ladder into the dinghy that would carry them ashore, she lost her grip on her bag. The bag and money went into the water and were lost. Fortunately, a fellow passenger gave the women enough money to continue their journey to Philadelphia. They arrived in Philadelphia on September 7, 1833.

The women found lodgings in a house in Willings Alley in the city through the help of another woman named Mrs. McDonogh. Mrs. McDonogh told the local pastor, Reverend Terence J. Donaghoe, about the Irish women who had come to serve the poor in Philadelphia. Father Donaghoe came to visit the women. He soon found a building which he could rent for them so that they could open their school. The school opened a few days later. The pupils were the daughters of Irish immigrants. The girls' parents were eager to have their daughters receive an education. Mary Frances and the others all took on work in one of the garment factories in order to support themselves during this time.

Father Donaghoe was also a strong supporter of education for the immigrant children. He believed education was the principal means by which the children would have better lives than their parents' lives of poverty. Father Donaghoe told the women that if they formed a religious society, they would all strengthen their own commitment to their cause and they would likely draw other women to join them. On November 1, with the approval of the Bishop of Philadelphia, the Congregation of the Sisters of Charity of the Blessed Virgin Mary was formed. The women took vows of poverty, chastity and obedience. They chose Mary Frances to be their leader, or the Mother of the group. Mary Frances, in turn, instructed the women to "teach without seeming to teach." She believed in the competence of the women who would lead the students.

A few months later, Rose O'Toole left Dublin to join the other women in Philadelphia. She carried 100 pounds in gold. She also brought necessities for the Sisters' house. The money was used to pay the rent on two more buildings for the school and for a separate convent. The first new members to the order entered in 1835. The Sisters moved again in 1837 when a larger convent was built as well as a boarding school.

In 1841, the Bishop of Dubuque, Iowa learned about the Sisters' work in Philadelphia. He was eager for the Sisters to come to the diocese of Dubuque which encompassed a great deal of the Upper Midwest Region. The area was opening to settlement. There were large indigenous populations throughout the region. The Bishop wanted the Sisters to help bring education and the Catholic faith to all of these people.

Five Sisters left Philadelphia in 1843. Bishop Loras of Dubuque accompanied them on their journey. Also traveling with them was the newly appointed Bishop of St. Louis, their old friend, Father, now Bishop Peter Richard Kendrick. The group traveled to Dubuque by train and then by riverboat on the Mississippi River. They reached Dubuque on June 23, 1843. Bishop Loras welcomed the Sisters to Dubuque.

The Sisters opened St. Mary Academy in Dubuque on July 5, 1843. The building was a simple log cabin. A few months later, Father Donaghoe, Mary Frances and the remaining Sisters in Philadelphia followed the others to Dubuque. Father Donaghoe returned to Philadelphia but soon felt it was best to leave because members of the 'Know Nothing Party' had burned St. Michael's Church, school and convent. The Party members had made it clear they did not want the priest, the Sisters or their school in Philadelphia.

The Sisters turned the Dubuque school into a boarding school so that more girls could receive an education. It was too far for many of the girls to walk to school each day. More women came to join the congregation as well. A regional motherhouse was built ten miles west of Dubuque. The motherhouse was called St. Joseph's Prairie Home. Four years later, fire completely destroyed St. Joseph's.

The Sisters built again, this time in the city of Dubuque. The Sisters continued to have more parish schools and more boarding schools built all along the "Mississippi River, eastward to Chicago, and westward along the Oregon and Santa Fe trails to San Francisco and Phoenix." The Sisters taught the children of new settlers, miners and traders. Mary Frances wrote letters to the Sisters in all of the towns where the congregation had schools. She reminded the Sisters to never turn any child away but to welcome all regardless of their circumstances or religious affiliations.

Mary Frances wrote letters to her family in Dublin as well. She learned through a letter that both of her parents had passed away. In 1852, she encouraged her own sisters and a niece to immigrate to Dubuque to join her. Her niece became one of the pupils in St. Joseph's Academy.

In 1862, Catherine Byrne passed away. She was the first of the original Dublin members to depart. When Father Donaghoe passed away in 1869, Mary Frances became the president of the entire congregation. She counted on the support of her Sisters, especially the women who comprised the original members of their congregation. Margaret Mann passed away in 1873. She was followed by Eliza Kelly in 1881. In 1883, The Sisters of Charity of the Blessed Virgin Mary celebrated fifty years as a congregation. Mary Frances was still the head of the congregation. She retained that role until her death at the age of eighty-five years on December 4, 1887. At the time of her death, Mary Frances and the Sisters had established schools in twenty-three towns throughout the Midwest as well as in San Francisco. Rose O'Toole was now the only one of the original five members still living. She passed away on March 10, 1890.

The Sisters provided an education for thousands of children. Many of the graduates of their schools became teachers who taught in the log cabin schoolhouses built wherever pioneering people settled. They were part of the foundation of the educational system forming in the United States in the 19th century. Mary Frances Clarke and her companions were tireless in their mission for equal access in education for all children.

KANSAS:
What a Woman Could Do

Catherine Devine McCarty Antrim

"Catherine Devine McCarty Antrim"
Courtesy Nita Stewart Haley Memorial Library

Women owned businesses were a rare sight in the 19th century in the western United States territories and states. Women managed homes and farms and ranches but they were rarely listed as the owners of a home or farm or ranch. Many women worked alongside their husbands in mercantile or grocery shops in towns, but they were not considered the owners of these establishments. Women were not seen at town council meetings very often. Life carried on under this norm for many women until a husband passed away. If a widow had no income of her own, or no family member to step in to provide for her and her children, she was destitute. Many widows found themselves in this position. They had to leave the old way of doing things behind them.

Catherine Devine was born around the year 1830 in Ireland. She immigrated to New York, leaving from Liverpool on the HMS *Devonshire* around 1848. She and Patrick Henry McCarty were married around the year 1851 in New York City. Catherine gave birth to a daughter, Bridget, in 1853. Her first son, William Henry McCarty, was born a few years later. Another son, Joseph, was born in 1863.

Patrick McCarty joined the Union Army during the U.S. Civil War. He lost his life during a battle in Pendleton County, Kentucky on May 25, 1865. Two years later, Catherine decided to move with her two sons to Indianapolis, Indiana. Her daughter Bridget was no longer with them. She found a house that she could afford and the family settled there. She also met a man named William Henry H. Antrim. He was living in a house near Catherine's house. William was a Union Army veteran who was now working as a teamster.

During this time, many pioneers were captivated by reports of gold and silver strikes in the West. People also learned that land for farming was available. Catherine and William decided to take her sons and move west. They migrated to Wichita, Kansas. The Kansas Territory had joined the Union in 1861. Wichita was a frontier town. Catherine secured a house for herself and her sons on the main street. William built a small house for himself six miles outside of Wichita. He planned to farm his land while also prospecting in the nearby area.

Catherine opened her own business in Wichita. She operated a hand washing laundry service from her house. The business was profitable. She began to take an interest in real estate. She decided to buy more property. Her sons were able to attend school. In July 1870, a meeting of the Wichita community was called. A petition was put forward to incorporate the town. There were 124 signers of the petition. The only woman to sign the petition was Catherine. William signed his name below Catherine's. The petition was approved by presiding Judge Reuben Riggs of Sedgwick County, Kansas.

In November of the same year, Catherine bought two parcels of land in her own name on Chisholm Street in Wichita. A few months later, she bought a quarter section of a lot next to William's land. The section cost $200. Catherine paid for the land in cash. She carried on with her laundry business and continued to make a profit.

Catherine suffered from tuberculosis. She had heard that many people with tuberculosis went to live in warm, dry climates which seemed to help them recover. Catherine and William decided that they should leave Wichita for a dryer climate. Catherine closed her laundry business and began to sell her properties. William sold his properties as well. The family migrated first to Denver, Colorado. Then they made their way to Santa Fe, New Mexico. They arrived in Santa Fe in the early months of 1873. On March 1, 1873, Catherine and William married. Catherine's two sons were the witnesses to the marriage.

The family did not remain in Santa Fe. They headed to Silver City, New Mexico where William wished to prospect for silver. He bought a small cabin for the family in Silver City. Catherine opened another laundry service in the home. She also baked and sold pies, cakes and bread. She took in boarders as well. Her sons were enrolled in the local school. One of her boarders remarked, "She kept boarders in Silver City, and her charity and goodness of heart was proverbial. Many a hungry tenderfoot has had cause to bless the fortune which led him to her door. In all her deportment she exhibited the unmistakable characteristics of a lady-a lady by instinct and education."

Catherine's income and William's intermittent income from mining and odd jobs kept the household finances stable. Living in a house was quite a luxury because many families in Silver City had only tents or rough shacks for their homes. Catherine managed her home and business on her own. She was a hard worker and determined to keep the family together. Unfortunately, the warm, dry air of New Mexico did not improve her tuberculosis. Catherine's health continued to deteriorate. Eventually, she was confined to her bed. Her son William stayed by her side, comforting her during her coughing spells. A neighbor, Clara Truesdell, a graduate of a nursing school, also tended to Catherine. Catherine confided to Clara that she was worried about what would happen to her sons when she died. Clara promised Catherine that she would look after the boys.

Catherine passed away on September 16, 1874. She was forty-five years old. Her husband William was away from home during her final months. He was not found in time to attend Catherine's funeral which took place in their home. Neighbors prepared her body and built a coffin for her and dug her grave. Catherine's two sons and the neighbors accompanied her body to the cemetery. They placed a simple wooden cross on her grave.

When William returned to Silver City, he learned that Catherine had died. He sold the cabin and placed his two stepsons with different families. He left Silver City and migrated to Arizona. William Henry and Joseph saw each other only infrequently. William Henry fell into criminal activities. His nickname was 'Billy the Kid'. Eventually, he became known as the 'most notorious outlaw in the West'. William died at the age of twenty-one years in 1881. Catherine's other son, Joseph, eventually settled in Colorado where he lived alone and in poverty. Catherine's worries for her sons that they would be alright after her death were prescient. She had managed for many years on her own, keeping them with her, housed, fed, clothed and safe. In a time when women rarely had control of their own money or destiny, Catherine had taken charge of her life and cared for her sons. She was a founding member of the town of Wichita. Catherine lived her life without regard for conventional thoughts about 'what a woman could do'.

KENTUCKY:
We Will Keep to Our Plan

Mary Ann Lynch McManus

In the year 1791, two Irish immigrants, Thomas and Mary Ann Lynch McManus, left Lancaster, Pennsylvania where they had been living since emigrating from Ireland. Mary Ann had given birth to four children in Lancaster since their arrival. The children were Margaret, Mary, Charles and Naomi, who was only a few months old. Along with a group of mostly other Irish immigrants, the McManus family was part of a group of Catholics who answered Bishop John Carroll's call for Catholics to set up Catholic colonies in the Kentucky Territory. There was already one such settlement composed of people who came from St. Mary's County, Maryland. Their group settled near Pottinger's Creek in Nelson County, Kentucky in 1785. Bishop Carroll wanted the group from Lancaster to settle in Bardstown, Kentucky. An earlier colony had arrived in Bardstown in 1787. Kentucky was the westernmost Territory in the state of Virginia at the time and was on the verge of gaining statehood.

The Lancaster group boarded a flatboat in Pittsburgh, Pennsylvania. The boat carried the group along the Ohio River. Near the town of Gallipoli, Ohio, the boat came under fire. Thomas McManus and some of the other men were killed. The attackers fled the scene, leaving the group devastated. The survivors secured the flatboat. Then they went ashore to bury the dead men. After this, they boarded the boat again and continued their journey. When they reached the town of Winchester in Clark County, Kentucky, they decided to settle there.

Mary Ann managed to find a house for herself and the children. She was resigned to staying in Winchester now that Thomas was gone. Only a short time later, the house caught fire and burned to the ground. Mary Ann and the children escaped but lost everything except for a few books. The neighbors around them offered to take in the family. Mary Ann, however, decided that she and the children should instead keep to their original plan and continue on to Bardstown. Somehow, she managed to get her family there. They arrived just after the new century began. Mary Ann was able to find work and a house for the family. The townspeople welcomed them. The community came together a few years later in order to build St. Joseph's Church. All of the townspeople, Catholics and non-Catholics came together for the dedication.

"St. Joseph Cathedral, formally the Basilica of Saint Joseph Proto Cathedral in Bardstown, Kentucky" Creator; Highsmith, Carol M., Courtesy Library of Congress Prints and Photographs Division LC-DIG-highsm-64133

Mary Ann became well known for her compassion and generosity towards others. The Honorable Benjamin J. Webb, one of Bardstown's residents, told a story about Mary Ann's generosity. "I remember to have heard when a boy, an edifying anecdote related of Mrs. McManus: One evening an immigrant family approached her cabin door and asked for food and shelter for the night. She was herself in great straits at the time, not knowing whence was to come the next day's supplies for herself and her little ones. At first she was much troubled, but her face soon brightened up, and she said: God will provide! In His name I bid you welcome."

The years passed and Mary Ann's children grew up. Her son Charles established himself as the leading merchant of Bardstown. He and Mary Ann Roby married and were prominent citizens of the town. Her daughter Mary married a man named Edward Hayden. Sadly, her youngest daughter, Naomi, passed away at the age of twenty-six in 1817. Mary Ann's grief over losing her daughter was great. Mary Ann lived to be sixty-three years old. She passed away in 1825. She was remembered as one of the founding members of the town, a woman who never lost her nerve and kept to the plan to make a home for her family in Bardstown, Kentucky.

LOUISIANA:

Angel of Orphaned Children

Margaret Gaffney Haughery

Orphaned children in the 1800s, whether in a city or in rural areas of the United States, were often tossed about by the winds of fate. Sometimes, relatives or neighbors stepped forward to take them in, or county officials placed them in orphanages. Some children were left completely on their own. Most adults thought it was best that orphaned children be gainfully employed. People thought that putting a child into a work environment would keep them away from those who would use them for criminal or nefarious purposes. They also thought by working, a child would not succumb to harmful temptations.

Margaret Gaffney was one of thousands of immigrant children left without any family while still a very young child. Margaret was born in 1813 to William and Margaret Gaffney who lived on a small farm with their other children in Tully South, Carrigallen, County Leitrim, Ireland. The Gaffneys were desperately poor. The family barely had enough to eat each day. After two years of very poor harvests, William and Margaret believed they could no longer provide for their children in Ireland. In 1818, they decided the family must immigrate to America. After selling nearly all they owned, they still did not have enough money for the entire family to immigrate. The difficult decision was made to leave the three oldest children in Ireland. William and Margaret and the three youngest children, Kevin, Margaret and Kathleen, would immigrate. William and Margaret planned to find work in America. They would save their money, then send for the other children. They left the oldest children with Margaret's brother, Matthew O'Rourke.

The ocean crossing was rough, but finally, the family reached Baltimore, Maryland. William and Margaret did find work, but they never earned enough money to send for their other children. Four years after their arrival in Baltimore, an epidemic of yellow fever took the lives of William and Margaret. Their youngest daughter, Kathleen, also fell victim to the disease. Margaret, aged nine years and her brother Kevin were left on their own. A woman who had sailed on the same ship with the Gaffneys took Margaret in to live at her house. Margaret never knew what happened to her brother.

In her new home, Margaret was expected to work hard to earn her keep. When she was old enough, she went into domestic service. She worked in houses in the Baltimore area. When she was twenty-four years old, she married Charles Haughery, another Irish immigrant. Shortly after their wedding on October 10, 1835, Margaret and Charles left Baltimore to seek their fortunes. They headed southwest, taking up residence in New Orleans, Louisiana. New Orleans was home to many immigrants from France who followed Catholicism. This made the town appealing to Irish Catholics as well.

The following year, Charles became ill. Margaret was expecting their first child. Charles returned to Ireland in hopes of regaining his health. Instead, he passed away shortly after reaching Ireland. Margaret gave birth to a daughter. She named the baby Frances. Frances did not survive infancy. Margaret was all alone now.

A woman on her own did not have many rights and very few protections in the 1830s. Margaret turned to a group of women religious, the Sisters of Charity, to help her find a way to earn an income and a place to live. The Sisters found work for Margaret. She became a laundress in the St. Charles Hotel. Margaret's work days were long and the work was grueling. Margaret was earning a wage that allowed her to live simply with some money left over. She gave the money to the Sisters to help them in their care of the city's orphans. The Sisters managed the Poydras Orphan Asylum. Margaret came to know some of the children in the orphanage when she began assisting the Sisters in their work. When she had saved enough money, she purchased two cows so the children would have fresh milk every day. She developed a strong business acumen while out securing donations for the children's care. Eventually, she was employed as the manager of the asylum.

Margaret decided to start her own dairy. The two cows she had purchased for the orphanage produced more milk than the children could consume in a day. So Margaret bought a cart. She traveled throughout the city selling the extra milk as well as butter and cheese. Margaret made quite a success of her small dairy business. She was able to save enough money to finance the building of a new orphanage for the children as well as another orphanage in a different part of the town. Margaret then bought a bakery shop. She named the bakery, 'Margaret Haughery & Company'. She sold bread from a cart as well as in the shop. This enterprise also became quite profitable. Margaret supplied all of the orphanages in New Orleans with bread. Every evening, she gave away leftover bread to the hungry poor people in the city.

During the U.S. Civil War years, Margaret, along with other business leaders, tried to help assuage some of the deprivations the residents of New Orleans were facing. She delivered bread each day to those in dire need of food. She did not distinguish between those who had once been affluent and those who were desperately poor. She did not distinguish between those who sympathized with Confederate or Union causes. Margaret became known as 'The Bread Woman'. She provided the funds for the building of seven more orphanages to care for the increasing numbers of children left alone due to the war or to epidemics of yellow fever. Margaret was known as 'The Mother of Orphans' and the 'Angel of the Delta'.

When she was sixty-nine years old, in 1882, Margaret became seriously ill. She passed away after several months. The Sisters of Charity were her nurses. Upon her death, the Times-Picayune of New Orleans printed her obituary on the front page of the newspaper, edged in black. She was given a state funeral which was attended by thousands of people. Among the attendees were dignitaries from government, religious institutions and businesses. The children of the orphanages attended as well as many who had once lived in the orphanages.

"Margaret Monument" Publisher: Detroit Publishing Co, between 1900-1906 Courtesy Library of Congress Prints and Photographs Division LC-DIG-Detroit-4a10799

In 1884, a monument to Margaret was placed at the intersection of Camp and Prytania Streets in New Orleans. The area was designated as 'Margaret's Place'. The monument was one of the first in the United States erected to the memory of a woman.

Margaret's lifework impacted thousands of lives. Her experiences of poverty, immigration and being orphaned at a very young age inspired her spirit of generosity and compassion. She gave away nearly all of her income to support those who could not support themselves. In her will, Margaret directed that any money remaining in her name should be divided among all of New Orleans's orphanages without regard to religious affiliation. For all of those children, Margaret was their angel.

MAINE:

A Life of Wealth and Generosity

Winifred Kavanagh

In the early years of the 19th century, women lived at home until they married. If they did not marry, they remained in the family home. Many of these women cared for aging parents or helped other family members with their children. Women who had means often did volunteer work and gave generously to charitable causes. Winifred Kavanagh was one such woman born into wealth and privilege. In her adult years, she contributed generously to many causes.

Winifred was born in 1806 to James and Sarah Jackson Kavanagh. Her father was an Irish immigrant who had traveled with his business partner, Matthew Cottrill, from Coolnamuck, Inistioge, County Kilkenny, Ireland. They left Ireland from the port at Wexford on a ship heading to Canada. From Canada, they made their way to Boston, Massachusetts in 1780. Eight years later they chose Newcastle, Maine as the site of their first business venture in America. They opened a general store which proved to be quite successful. The men next built a lumber mill, a grist mill and a fulling mill(for strengthening and waterproofing woolen fabric) near Damariscotta Lake. They employed workers to build ships for transporting lumber. The new establishments led to the village which grew up around all of this industry, Damariscotta Mills.

By the year 1803, both men decided that they would have houses built which befitted their affluence. They were the richest men in the area so cost was not a hindrance. They hired another Irish immigrant, Nicholas Codd, to design and build their homes. When Winifred Kavanagh was born in 1806, in addition to her parents, there were already six children living in the grand Federal style home Nicholas Codd had designed. Winifred grew up in this house surrounded by family and all of the comforts her father's wealth enabled.

James and Matthew were devout Catholics who got along well with their mostly Protestant neighbors. As more Catholics migrated to the area, the two men wanted to have a stalwart Catholic Church in their community rather than the wooden structure currently in use. In 1807, the two men donated the money to build a new Catholic Church. Nicholas Codd was once again hired to design and build the church. The bricks were manufactured nearby, then hauled across the frozen Damariscotta River. The lime used for the mortar was imported from Ireland. The church was finished within one year and still stands today as the oldest Catholic Church in the New England region. In addition to attending Mass, all of the Kavanagh children were sent to schools run by religious orders. Winifred was sent to school in Boston.

Sarah Kavanagh passed away at the age of thirty-seven years in 1813. Winifred was seven years old. She was cared for by her two older sisters, Sarah and Margaret. When she was not at school, Winifred lived at home. She grew up in wealth even though her father's businesses suffered setbacks after the war years of 1812-1815.

James Kavanagh passed away in 1828. Winifred's brother Edward, who had intended to take over his father's businesses, instead entered politics. He was a member of the Maine legislature and then was assigned the position of the charge d'affaires to Portugal. Edward served in this capacity from 1835-1841. During this time Winifred lived in Portugal with Edward for eighteen months. Other than this time, Winifred lived at home. When Edward became the Governor of Maine in 1843, Winifred supported him in many ways. Edward suffered from rheumatism which left him weak and in constant pain. Winifred helped to nurse Edward. She was the executor of Edward's will when he died in 1844 after only ten months in office.

Winifred did not marry. She chose instead, to focus her time and money on compassionate causes and in support of the education of girls. In 1877, she donated $25,000 for the building of the Kavanagh School in Portland, Maine which was run by the Sisters of Charity. She donated $25,000 to the Catholic Orphan Asylum in Whitfield, Maine. She did not limit her charitable contributions to Catholic causes, but gave generously to many charities regardless of religious affiliation. Winifred also kept watch over her many nieces and nephews. At different times, she had some of her nieces living with her.

Bishop's Residence and Kavanagh School Courtesy Maine Historical Society

Winifred passed away at the age of seventy-seven years on November 4, 1883. She had suffered a stroke a few weeks earlier which left her paralyzed. Her will included many bequests for her family members. All of her nieces were to inherit the contents of her home while all of her nephews were to share equally in her real estate holdings. She left a considerable fortune to her nieces in stocks as well. She was remembered as a woman of great charity and grace. None of the biographies of her entrepreneurial father or her political brother mentioned Winifred. She did not live flamboyantly and so was not often mentioned in the newspapers of the time. Although usually without publicity, Winifred was highly regarded by those who received her patronage. Wealth did not bring her fame but it did allow her opportunities to benefit others.

MARYLAND:

Taking on the Railroad

Hannah Dougherty

Hannah Dougherty was born in 1830 in Ireland. She immigrated to the United States around the year 1850. The ship Hannah sailed on came into port in Baltimore, Maryland. Next to New York City, the port at Baltimore received the largest number of Irish immigrants. James Dougherty also emigrated from Ireland at around the same time. He was born in 1828. Hannah and James met and eventually married. They came to live in a part of Baltimore known as Irishtown. Near Irishtown was the Mt. Clare Station of the Baltimore & Ohio Railroad.

In 1860, James was working as a hostler. A hostler minded the horses for people who were staying in a hotel or inn. The job did not pay much

"Transportation Engines"
Courtesy Library of Congress Prints and Photographs Division LC-USE6-D-006810

money. Like many Irish immigrant men, the jobs available to them were mostly low paying and did not require skilled labor. Hannah and James already had welcomed three sons into their family by 1860. James needed a different job that paid better wages. He found work with the B & O Railroad Company. Many Irish immigrants stepped directly from the ships which had carried them across the ocean into jobs with this railroad.

The B & O Railroad Company first began laying tracks in 1832. Eastern railroad company owners realized that they would need to lay tracks west from the East Coast into the Midwest region of the country in order to transport goods, grains and produce in a timely manner. Already with the completion of the Erie Canal in 1825 and other canal projects, the time it took to ferry products via canals had greatly reduced shipment times, thus enticing farmers and merchants to utilize canal transport. Railroad company owners did not want to miss out on the profits to be had by rail shipping. There was a continual need for workers to build rail tracks, maintain the tracks, load and unload freight and to operate the trains. Thousands of Irish immigrants filled these needs. In general, railroad owners preferred to hire recent immigrants because they knew that most of these people needed work immediately. They also knew that immigrants were unlikely to complain about low wages and long hours. These workers would not be put off by the dangerous nature of the work: using explosives to blast through rock, hammering iron spikes into the tracks without wearing any protective gear, working in and around moving train cars and loading wood and coal into fireboxes.

James worked as a laborer near where the B & O trains ran through Sykesville, Maryland. One day, he was struck and killed by some passing train cars. His death left Hannah with six children to raise on her own. Andrew, the eldest, was twelve years old. Edward and James were ten and eight years old. The twins, Hannah and Sarah were only four years old. The youngest, Mary, was an infant. James's income was the only money the family had. They had no savings.

Hannah could neither read nor write. Her days were filled with housekeeping duties and tending to the needs of her children. She and the children attended Mass on Sundays but otherwise did not enjoy social activities in the town. Hannah needed a way to earn money to keep her family together but her options were limited. To her great surprise, one year after James's death, Hannah learned that the State of Maryland, on her behalf, was going to sue the B & O Railroad Company for compensation due to her and her children stemming from James's death.

The Baltimore Sun Newspaper reported on the case in the December 18, 1869 issue. The case put before Judge Dobbins read, "The State of Maryland, use of Hannah Dougherty, widow, & c., vs the Baltimore and Ohio Railroad Company, action to recover ten thousand dollars for alleged injuries to James Dougherty, by defendants's cars, at Sykesville, October 13th, 1868, from which injuries said Dougherty died; on trial." Three days later, the Baltimore Sun again mentioned the trial. On December 21st, it was reported "Argued by Judge Merrill and H.V.D. Johns, Esq., for plaintiffs, and F.C. Latrobe and J.Randolph Tucker's for defendant. Juryout." The next day, December 22, 1869, the Baltimore Sun reported, "Damages for Causing Death. In the Superior Court, yesterday, before Judge Dobbin, in the case of Hannah Dougherty, widow, and six children, against the Baltimore and Ohio Railroad Company, being an action to recover damages for the killing of James Dougherty, a laborer, by the locomotive of the defendant, at Sykesville, Carroll County, October 13th, 1868, the jury, after being out all Monday night and part of yesterday, returned a verdict for plaintiff for $4000, apportioned as follows: To Hannah Dougherty, widow of James Dougherty, $1000, and to the children as follows: Andrew, $350: Edward, $400: James, $450: Hannah, $525: Sarah, $525: and Mary, $750. The defendants filed a motion for a new trial."

In September of the following year, 1870, the second trial commenced. Counsel for the plaintiffs and defendant appeared before Judge Dobbin in Superior Court once again. The court was adjourned for the day so the next report from the Baltimore Sun appeared on Saturday, October 1, 1870. The only news was that the jury was deliberating. On Tuesday, October 4, 1870, the headline in the newspaper read, "Ten Thousand Dollars Damages". The article again reported that the case came before Judge Dobbin to recover damages for the killing of James by the defendant's cars. The jury returned the verdict for the plaintiff as follows: "To Hannah Dougherty, widow, $3000: to her six children, Andrew, $628.18: Edward, $807.68: James, $987.14: Hannah, $1,435.84: Sarah, $1,435.84: Mary, $1,705.34-total $10,000. The counsel for the defendant, Messrs. Latrobe & Son, filed a motion for a new trial"

During the years of the trial and the waiting period before the monetary compensation was disbursed, Hannah, Andrew and her three daughters were living in Carroll, Maryland. Without income to keep the family together, Hannah had placed Edward and James with other families. The boys were living near the town of Libertytown. James worked as an errand boy. When Hannah finally did receive the settlement, she used the money to buy 185 acres of land near Eldersburg, Maryland. She and the children planned to farm the land. Ten years later, Hannah and all of the children except for James, were living on the farm. The farm's assessed worth was approximately $4000. The 1880 agricultural census presented a listing of the farm's assets and earnings for 1879. "$950 worth of goods, (possibly from the sale of 450 pounds of butter, 600 dozen eggs plus other products.) There were five horses, two mules, 18 cows(including six milch cows), seven pigs, 50 chickens and an orchard of apple and peach trees."

Hannah's son, Andrew, passed away on April 11, 1895. He was thirty-nine years old. Without Andrew to help with running the farm, Hannah was at a loss for how to keep the farm going. Hannah's youngest daughter passed away in 1898. After her death, Hannah began selling off parcels of the land. Edward and James no longer lived on the farm. Hannah, with her daughters Sarah and Hannah, moved to Freeland, Maryland. They lived together until Hannah's death in 1901 at the age of seventy years. Hannah's will listed $813.24 lodged in the Farmers and Mechanics National Bank of Westminster. She also had $210 at home. An Irish immigrant of no independent means had stood up to the B & O Railroad Company in order to keep her family together and to provide for their security.

MASSACHUSETTS:
Kitchen Chats and Poetry Scraps

Margaret Maher

I'm Nobody! Who are you?

By

Emily Dickinson

I'm nobody! Who are you?

Are you nobody, too?

Then there's a pair of us—don't tell!

They'd banish us, you know.

How dreary to be somebody!

How public, like a frog

To tell your name the livelong day

To an admiring bog!

"I'm Nobody Who Are You?"
Author: Emily Dickinson Public Domain

The poet, Emily Dickinson, 1830-1886, is recognized as one of the greatest American poets of the 19th century. She wrote as many as 1,800 poems although only seven of these were published before her death at the age of fifty-six years. For most of her life, she lived in Amherst, Massachusetts in the family home with her parents, Edward and Emily Norcross Dickinson, her brother Austin and sister Lavinia. The Dickinsons were affluent and well-known in Amherst society. They employed domestic workers and outside laborers to maintain their grand home, gardens and farm. One woman, Margaret Maher, an Irish immigrant, was in the employ of the Dickinson family for thirty years. In a time when servants were expected to be unseen and unheard, Margaret and Emily disregarded that convention. It is primarily due to Margaret's admiration for Emily that the collected works of Emily Dickinson are known today.

Margaret Maher was born in Killusty, County Tipperary in 1841. Her parents were Michael and Mary Dunne Maher. There were three other children in the family: Mary, born in 1828, Michael, born in 1843 and Thomas, born in 1848. The three older Maher children immigrated to the United States in 1854. They made their way to Amherst, Massachusetts and settled there. Mary Maher married a man named Thomas Kelley, another immigrant from County Tipperary. Michael Maher eventually set out for California to work in the gold mines. Two years after the Maher siblings sailed for America, Margaret returned to Tipperary. She had come to collect her parents and younger brother Thomas. The four Mahers safely crossed the Atlantic Ocean and came to settle in Amherst as well.

Margaret found work as a domestic servant in the home of Fanny and Lucius Boltwood in Amherst. She then transferred her work to the home of their son Lucius in 1861 when he and his wife Clarissa were expecting their first child. Margaret remained with the Boltwood family until 1868. She moved with them to Washington, D. C., and then to Hartford, Connecticut. She returned to Amherst in 1868 in order to care for her ailing father. Her mother had already passed away. Michael Maher died on June 8, 1868. Five days later, Margaret's brother-in-law fell from a great height at the factory in town where he was employed. Margaret remained in Amherst to help her sister care for Thomas throughout the summer months. Gradually, Thomas recovered though he had lost one arm.

With Thomas out of danger, Margaret made plans to travel with her brother Thomas to California. She planned to open a boarding house near where her brother Michael was working. Thomas was eager to make his fortune in California. On October 5, 1868, Thomas left for California alone. Margaret could not travel with him because she was suffering from typhus. Her sister Mary nursed her through many long days. When Margaret was finally recovered, she once again began planning her trip to California. She took on temporary work as a domestic servant in order to accumulate the money for her journey.

Margaret went to work in Amherst for a woman named Mrs. Talcott. One day, she was approached by Edward Dickinson. He wanted to know when Margaret could begin working for his family as an 'all-in-one' maid. Margaret explained that she was only taking on temporary work since she would be leaving the next year in May. Edward Dickinson promised an increase in her wages if she would come to work for his family. Margaret agreed and moved to the Dickinson home in March 1869. Even though she 'lived in' with the Dickinsons, Margaret considered Mary and Thomas's house to be her home.

Margaret was employed by the Dickinson family for the next thirty years. She was in charge of everything related to the running of the household. Her daily work included preparing all of the meals, laying tables for dining, seeing to the needs of the household members and their many guests, cleaning house, laying fires, clearing ashes, mending, washing and ironing. Fortunately, some of the daily chores were carried out by the Dickinson sisters. Emily and Lavinia's parents subscribed to the popular idea of the time that household work for the daughters of wealthy members of society was necessary for their moral and spiritual growth. Emily chose to do most of the daily baking while Lavinia chose dusting the many rooms.

While Emily was mixing bread dough and baking tarts, Margaret was washing pots and dishes and cleaning and cooking the daily meals. The two women spent hours together in the kitchen. Over the years, they came to know each other well. Emily insisted upon calling Margaret 'Maggie', a name Margaret did not favor. The entire household came to refer to Margaret as Maggie. Sometimes, Emily teased Margaret. She would, at times, make belittling remarks about Margaret being Irish and about Irish immigrants in general. This was not an uncommon practice among wealthy families at the time. Yet, Emily considered Margaret to be the bright spot in the family home. Margaret was very protective of Emily. As the years passed, Emily became reclusive to the point of no longer leaving the house. Sometimes, Emily did not come out of her bedroom for days. She was a prolific letter writer even during these times. She corresponded with many people. Margaret found herself passing letters back and forth from Emily and her many respondents in Amherst. She posted letters Emily had written to out of town acquaintances nearly every day.

Emily often wrote short lines of verse on whatever scrap of paper she found at hand. Margaret would find these scraps in the pockets of Emily's dresses or scattered among the pages of books. She saved the scraps. She also saved the small booklets of poetry that Emily assembled. Margaret placed the writings in the trunk she had brought with her from Ireland. She kept the trunk in her room. She did not tell anyone that she saved Emily's writings.

Margaret nursed Emily throughout her life in Amherst. Emily was bothered by weak eyes and suffered from damaged lungs. Her final illness left her weak and gasping for breath. Emily begged Margaret to burn all of her writings upon her death. She extracted the same promise from her sister Lavinia regarding the collected letters from acquaintances and relatives. When Emily passed away on May 15, 1886, Margaret encountered a dilemma. Should she honor Emily's wishes by burning all of the collected poems written on the scraps of paper in her trunk? Or should she make their presence known? Margaret decided to ignore Emily's wishes. She gave the collection of papers to Lavinia.

Lavinia decided Emily's poems should be published. The first collection of Emily's poetry appeared in 1890. The collection was well received locally and then beyond Amherst. The number of people who admired Emily's work grew every year.

Margaret remained in the Dickinson household for seventeen more years. When Lavinia passed away in 1899, Margaret was fifty-eight years old. It was time for her to leave the Dickinson home. Her brother-in-law Thomas had a house built for Margaret on property adjoining his house. Margaret moved in and opened a boarding house. The property with the two houses became known as Kelley Square. Mary Kelley passed away in 1910. Thomas died in 1920. Their children continued to care for Margaret in her later years. The scraps of Emily's poems that Margaret saved are, in part, Margaret's legacy as well as the treasured legacy of Emily Dickinson.

MICHIGAN:

The Sound the Stars Make Rushing through the Sky

Bamewawagezhikaquay, Jane Johnston Schoolcraft

"Jane Johnston Schoolcraft" Johnston Family Papers HS 156 Bentley Historical Library, University of Michigan

Jane Johnston was born in Sault Ste. Marie, Michigan on January 31, 1800. She was the daughter of John Johnston and Ozhaguscodawayquay, also known as Susan Johnston. Ozhaguscodawayquay was the daughter of the Ojibwe Chief Waubojeeg. Jane was the eldest daughter of eight children. Jane's parents built a trading post in Sault Ste. Marie. They dealt in furs and thus, came to be well known among the fur trappers and traders, as well as the local indigenous community.

Jane's father, John Johnston, was born in 1762 in Belfast, Ireland. His family owned an estate, Craigballynoe, near the town of Coleraine, on the border between Counties Derry and Antrim. Eventually, John held the title for the vast estate. As a young man, however, he became interested in the fur trade which was booming in North America. He sailed for Montreal in 1790, hoping to make his fortune. Upon his arrival in Montreal, John became acquainted with the owners of the Northwest Company of Montreal, dealers in furs. Upon joining the company, John headed for Sault Ste. Marie, in the Michigan Territory. John began trading in furs. He met the Ojibwe Chief Waubojeeg who was chief of the 'North Shore of Lake Huron and both shores of Lake Superior'.

Jane's mother, Ozhaguscodawayquay, was a much loved daughter. She was a great storyteller, and much revered, just like her father. When Chief Waubojeeg noticed that John Johnston was interested in

Ozhaguscodawayquay, he became wary. He had known French and English fur traders who married indigenous women, only to desert them, often leaving them with small children and no provision for their care. Instead of agreeing to John's request to marry Ozhaguscodawayquay, Chief Waubojeeg told John to return to Montreal. If after staying away for the winter, John returned to Sault Ste. Marie, then he would give his consent for John to marry his daughter. John did as the chief requested. When he returned to Sault Ste. Marie, John and Ozhaguscodawayquay were married.

When Jane was born, her parents gave her the Ojibwe name, Bamewawagezhikaquay. Her name meant, 'the sound the stars make rushing through the sky'. Her English language name would be Jane. Jane received her education from both of her parents. Ozhaguscodawayquay understood the English language but conversed only in her native Ojibwe language. Jane grew up speaking both languages fluently. Ozhaguscodawayquay also taught Jane traditional household duties and needlework. She shared Ojibwe stories with Jane. John had brought with him an extensive library of books when he immigrated to North America. He shared these with Jane, teaching her the English language as well as the French language. Jane learned to read and write and studied the Bible as well as classical literature. She shared a love of history and poetry with her father.

During the winter of 1809-1810, Jane traveled with her father to Ireland because he had to deal with business matters concerning his estate. In order to continue her education, John sent Jane to stay with his sister and her husband, John and Jane Johnston Moore at their home in County Wexford. During her stay, Jane's Uncle John Moore passed away. Jane's father traveled to the Moore home in order to collect Jane lest the burden of another mouth to feed be too great for his sister. He and Jane traveled to England before returning to Sault Ste. Marie.

When Jane was twenty years old, she met Henry Rowe Schoolcraft. Schoolcraft was traveling with the Michigan Territorial Governor, Lewis Cass, to Sault Ste. Marie. Governor Cass wished to establish a fort at Sault Ste. Marie to protect both Michigan's and the United States' interests after the War of 1812 against England ended. Also traveling with the Governor were soldiers the governor wanted stationed in the new fort. The Johnstons welcomed the Governor and Henry Schoolcraft into their home. Jane and Henry became acquainted. Jane's poise and demeanor, as well as her intelligence and knowledge, interested Schoolcraft greatly. He was interested in learning as much as he could about the Ojibwe people. He realized that Jane would be a great source of knowledge for his studies.

Jane and Henry married in 1823, one year after Henry was appointed the Indian Agent to the Michigan Territory. Their first son was born the following year. He was Panaysee, Little Bird. His English language name was William Henry. One year later, Jane gave birth to a stillborn daughter. Panaysee died at the age of three years, causing Jane great sadness. Happily, two more children, Jane Susan and John, were born in the following years. These two children grew to adulthood.

Jane, her mother and her siblings, taught Henry the Ojibwe language. They also shared the traditions of their tribe as well as the stories passed down through the generations. Henry wanted those stories written down. He planned to make the stories accessible to non-indigenous people. He believed the stories had literary value. Jane assisted Henry in this work of writing, translating and preserving the Ojibwe stories. The stories reflected Ojibwe values of truth, loyalty and the importance of remaining connected to family.

In 1826, Jane and Henry began to produce a literary magazine called *The Literary Voyager* or *Muzzenyegun*. Fourteen issues were eventually produced. The magazine contained traditional stories of the Ojibwe people as well as original stories written by Jane. Henry did not give Jane much credit for her work. He listed her stories with pseudonyms instead of Jane's own name. Two of the pseudonyms Henry used for Jane were 'Rosa' and 'Leelinau'. The magazine was well received. It was read by people in the Michigan Territory as well as by people as far away as New York.

In 1833, Jane and Henry and their two children went to live on Mackinac Island. A few years later, Henry was appointed the Superintendent for Indian Affairs by President Andrew Jackson. He was often away from home for months at a time. Jane struggled with poor health after the births of her children. She carried on as best she could but she became increasingly frail. Eventually, the doctor she visited prescribed laudanum to relieve her symptoms. Laudanum, derived from opium, was routinely prescribed for people in pain, as a cough suppressant, for insomnia and for a wide range of other ailments. Unfortunately, it was unknown at the time that the drug was highly addictive. Addiction to laudanum compounded Jane's ill health.

Henry lost his federal appointment as Superintendent of Indian Affairs in 1841 when charges of misconduct were leveled against him. He and Jane moved to New York City. The next year, Henry decided that they should travel to Europe where he hoped to promote his writings. Jane did not feel that she could make the trip to Europe. Instead, she traveled to Dundas, Ontario, Canada where her sister Charlotte was living. One day, Charlotte came into a room and found that Jane, sitting in a chair, had passed away. Jane was forty-two years old.

Jane's influence and her shared mission to keep the oral tradition of the Ojibwe people alive, did not end with her death. Influential writers that she had met while married to Henry often came to the Schoolcraft home. Their social circle was wide and diverse. One of these writers was Henry Wadsworth Longfellow. He was impressed with the work that Henry had done in translating the stories of the culture and the traditions of the Ojibwe people. He used much of what he learned from Jane and Henry in his epic poem, *Hiawatha*, published in 1865. Longfellow dedicated the poem to Henry Schoolcraft, never knowing that it was Jane who had furnished the translations of stories. It was Jane who recounted the traditions and described the culture of her Ojibwe family. Jane's dedication to preserving the Ojibwe culture earned her posthumously, the title 'First Woman of Native American Literature'.

MINNESOTA:

Tailor-made for the American Dream

Mary Theresa Mehegan Hill

"Mary Theresa Mehegan Hill"
Courtesy Minnesota Historical Society

Mary Theresa Mehegan was born in New York City, on the lower West Side. She was the daughter of Timothy and Mary McGowan Mehegan. Timothy emigrated from Ireland in the early 1840s. He was a tailor. He opened a shop once he reached New York City. He met Mary McGowan, who was also an Irish immigrant, in New York City. They married in 1844. Mary gave birth to Mary Theresa on July 1, 1846.

Working as a tailor did not provide enough steady income for the family to survive in the city. Timothy decided to move his family west to Chicago in 1847. The family remained in Chicago for three years. A second daughter, Anna Eliza, was born there in 1849. Tailoring did not make ends meet in Chicago either so the family moved again. This time, Timothy purchased a tract of land, sight unseen, in the Minnesota Territory. The family moved to their land, near St. Anthony Falls, Minnesota in May 1850. Unfortunately, Timothy soon found out that the land was poor and unfit for farming.

The family moved one last time. Timothy found a house for them on Bench Street, near the Mississippi River in the town of St. Paul, Minnesota. There were not many settlers living in St. Paul yet, but there was a Catholic chapel which suited the Catholic Mehegans very well. Once again, Timothy advertised his tailoring skills. He also sold real estate. Neither venture proved successful, though Timothy persevered for four years. On December 24, 1854, Timothy died suddenly. Mary and her two daughters were left without a penny to their names.

Mary struggled for two years to provide for her daughters. She married again, in 1856, to a man named Patrick Mulligan. The new family moved to a different house where two more daughters were born over the next few years. Mary Theresa and Anna began attending school at St. Joseph's Academy, run by the Sisters of St. Joseph. The two girls were among the very first to be enrolled when the academy opened.

During her teenage years, Mary Theresa worked in the Merchants Hotel in St. Paul. She served in the dining room of the hotel. One of the patrons of the hotel was a young man named James J. Hill. He often ate at the hotel because it was near his place of work at Boris and Champlin, a shipping agency. James was rising through the ranks of the company. He was a hard worker who wanted to learn all that he could about shipping and rail freight. His employers were pleased with his work. James came to know the businessmen of St. Paul as well. He planned to save his money until he could open his own shipping office.

Mary and James decided to marry. James was not a Catholic so their plans were not met with approval by everyone. Mary turned to her good friend, Father Louis Caillet. Father Caillet had often counseled Mary since the death of her father. He did not approve of Mary's marriage plans but told her that she should continue to educate herself so that she would be a good companion for James. When James heard about this, he and some friends of his paid the tuition for Mary to continue her education at St. Mary's Institute in Milwaukee, Wisconsin. Mary left for Milwaukee where she studied French, history, music, exercise, needlework, tapestry, crochet and knitting. Mary remained in Milwaukee for three years.

While Mary was away at school, James kept himself very busy. He began to offer his own services for freight contracts. He also sold coal. James began to make a name for himself in the shipping business. By the time Mary returned from Milwaukee, James had saved enough money for them to begin married life. On August 19, 1867, James and Mary married. Their first home was on Pearl Street in the area known as Lowertown, in St. Paul.

A few years later, James and associates decided to launch the Red River Transportation Company. The company provided steamboat transport between St. Paul, Minnesota and Winnipeg, Canada. James's coal interests had grown considerably. He was the only person selling anthracite coal in the expanding St. Paul area. He decided to expand into the banking business. He bought failing businesses in order to make them profitable and then sold them again, making a substantial profit in these deals.

In 1873, there was an economic panic which negatively impacted many railroad companies. James was particularly interested in the St. Paul and Pacific Railroad which had declared bankruptcy. James found three associates who agreed to buy the railroad with him. The men bought the railroad company and then set out to expand its route. They successfully acquired the rights to lay more track lines. The new railroad became known as the St. Paul, Minneapolis, and Manitoba Railway Company. James was the general manager.

Meanwhile, at home, Mary took care of the growing number of children born into their family. Ten children were born between 1868-1885. All but one of the children grew to adulthood. As the wife of an industrialist who was becoming more well known each day, Mary was expected to take her place in St. Paul and Minneapolis society. She and James did not entertain lavishly in the evenings, but they often held lunchtime soirées. It was required of Mary that she go visiting the other society women as well as have them visit in her home. Mary's calling cards stated that 'she was at home on Tuesday afternoons'. Mary understood that it was important that she appear composed and well turned out in order to advance James's business endeavors. It was equally important that the Hill home was immaculately kept and the children were always polite and deferential.

The endeavors that Mary enjoyed most were her own work in the Catholic schools and charities she supported. She taught knitting and sewing classes in schools run by the Sisters. She and James gave generously to the Catholic Church and to the schools. Mary also prepared the weekly menus for her household. She enjoyed preparing special dishes and took care of the household linens.

James continued to increase his rail holdings. He became known as 'the Empire Builder'. By the year 1889, James had railroads from Minnesota to Wisconsin and from Minnesota to North Dakota. His great vision was a transcontinental railroad that would extend from St. Paul, Minnesota all the way to Seattle, Washington. That rail line, known as the Great Northern Railway, was completed in 1893.

Mary's health began to trouble her only a few years into her married life. She was susceptible to bronchitis. She was diagnosed with tuberculosis when she was forty years old. She began to spend the winter months in the South where mild weather gave her some relief. James bought property on Jekyll Island, off the coast of Georgia. Jekyll Island was the wintertime retreat for the wealthiest industrialists of the time. Membership was extremely costly and closely monitored. Unofficially, the Jekyll Island Club was known as the Millionaires Club. Mary also began spending time in New York City during the winter months because the weather was less brutal than in St. Paul.

With James's wealth soaring, the family moved to a 36,000 square foot mansion on St. Paul's most prestigious street, Summit Street. The house was equipped with electric lighting. There were thirteen bathrooms, all with indoor plumbing. There was an art gallery and an impressive pixie organ. In addition to the Hill children growing up in the house, many influential businessmen, legislators, governors and even President William McKinley visited the home. Mary was in charge of everything concerned with the house. James was away from home over six months of the year overseeing his rail lines. When he was in town, he often worked in his office until late at night.

Mary held the city of St. Paul and all of Minnesota close to her heart. Every year she had a new doormat placed at the front door on the anniversary of the day she and her family arrived in Minnesota. She wrote in her diary from May 21, 1901, "Fifty-one years ago I arrived in St. Paul, then a little village, now a City of nearly two hundred thousand. Then but four hundred I believe-What changes. I was three, not fifty-four, from a little child to a grandmother. St. Paul has the advantage-it still grows."

James passed away in 1916 after years of declining health. Upon his death, James's wealth was estimated to be $63,000,000. Mary carried on with her daily duties and seasonal travel. She continued to give generously to her favorite charities. She and James had endowed a library in St. Paul. She arranged a number of trusts for various institutions.

She was one of the most influential people in the city. A high school was named in her honor in St. Paul in thanks for her philanthropy.

Mary Theresa Mehegan Hill passed away on November 22, 1921. She was seventy-five years old. Her well attended funeral was held in the Cathedral of St. Paul. She was laid to rest next to James in a plot on their family farm, known as North Oaks. Their graves were later moved to the Hill Family Plot in Resurrection Cemetery in Mendoza Heights, Minnesota. Mary Theresa was tailor-made for the American Dream.

MISSISSIPPI:
The Healing Touch

Mary Greenleaf Castles Willis

In the year 1822, the ship, *Caledonian*, left from the port in Belfast, Ireland to cross the Atlantic Ocean to the United States. On December 22 of that year, the ship reached the port at Charleston, South Carolina. Aboard the ship was a group of Irish immigrants who wanted to begin new lives in America. The group consisted mainly of families with very young children and single young men. One of these families was the Thomas Castles family. Thomas and his wife Mary Ann Greenleaf Castle were sailing with their three young daughters, Sarah, Eliza and Mary. Thomas, born in 1782 and Mary, born around the same time, were from Lisburn, County Antrim, Ireland. Mary's brother John was also traveling with them.

The new arrivals settled in Fairfield County, South Carolina for a few years. In 1827, many from the group migrated to Greene County, Alabama. Some of the men had received grants for land in Boligee, Alabama so they began farming there. William Willis, another of the group, had been twenty-four years old when he first arrived. He was now twenty-nine years old and the holder of four of these land grants. When Thomas Castles died that year, William stepped in to take care of Mary and her four daughters. He and Mary married a few months after Thomas's death.

William farmed the land he owned in Boligee. But after a few years, he, along with some of the others in their group, decided to migrate again. This time, they settled in Neshoba County, a part of which, in time, came to be organized as Newton County, Mississippi. William's brother Daniel, who had arrived on a later ship, moved with them to Mississippi in 1835. All of the immigrants settled on land near each other. As Mary's daughters grew up, some of them married men who owned land in the settlement. The settlement began to grow as the farms prospered. Families sent for their siblings, cousins and neighbors back in Ireland to join them. Many of Mary's relatives from her first marriage to Thomas also immigrated and settled in Newton County. With so many immigrants arriving, it was decided that a church must be built. William Willis donated the land for the Erin Cumberland Presbyterian Church. The next church that was built was called the New Ireland Baptist Church. The communities around both of these churches came to be known as Erin and New Ireland.

"Herbs" Photographer Isle Orsel
Public Domain through Unsplash

Mary fulfilled her duties in housekeeping, raising her children and helping with the farming. She gave birth to two more children after her marriage to William but neither child survived infancy. Mary was often called upon to assist other women in childbirth. Her neighbors looked to her to tend to anyone who was ill or injured. Many people thought of Mary as a physician even though she had never received any formal training. Mary was listed on the 1850 census form for Newton County as 'physician'. She was the first woman physician in Newton County and among the first physicians who served in Mississippi. Mary's treatments included the use of herbs for healing as well as other homeopathic remedies. She knew firsthand about the fragility of life. She devoted herself to relieving suffering and facilitating the healing of anyone who called upon her. Mary Greenleaf Castles Willis, self-taught physician, exemplified as best she could, the credo of formally trained physicians, "Do no harm" with her healing touch. She passed away around the year 1851 and was buried in the Erin Cumberland Presbyterian Church Cemetery in Newton County, Mississippi.

MISSOURI:
Leading by Example

Johanna Collins Redner Tobin

"Johanna Collins Tobin" Courtesy Stephen H. Hart Research Center at History Colorado

Many of the children of Irish immigrants in the 19th century went on to live fruitful and productive lives. Some even became quite famous. The parents of these children were thankful that they had brought their children to a place where opportunities for lives beyond poverty and despair were within their grasp. The most famous and celebrated of these immigrant offspring found their stories recounted in not just local newspapers, but national and even international newspapers. One such daughter of Irish immigrants became the talk of the nation due to a situation she had not instigated but became an integral part of all the same. Her name was Margaret Tobin Brown. Most know her today by the name gifted to her.. the unsinkable Molly Brown. The story of Margaret's mother, Johanna Collins Tobin, is equally important to that of Margaret's story, in part, because Johanna lived a life not in the spotlight. Her fame derived from the foundation she provided for her children, especially her daughter Margaret.

Johanna Collins was born in County Roscommon, Ireland in 1825. She was the daughter of Daniel and Margaret Collins. Her family immigrated to Pennsylvania while Johanna was still a very young child. She grew up in a family that supported Irish independence from

England's rule. She was aware that people's opinions about social class were deeply entrenched and not easily changed. Johanna was taught to think of all people as equal regardless of income or profession.

When Johanna was twenty-one years old, she married a man named William Redner. Johanna and William relocated to Davenport, Iowa. Their daughter Mary Ann was born in Davenport. While Mary Ann was still an infant, William passed away. Johanna had no assets and no plan for earning money.

Johanna accepted an invitation from her sister, Mary O'Leary, to come to Hannibal, Missouri where she was living. Johanna packed her things and the few belongings of her baby and moved to Hannibal. There was a large settlement of Irish immigrants in Hannibal. Most of these people were living in the part of the town known as 'Irish Shanty Town'. Johanna found herself surrounded by people who shared her same history. Mary accepted a position teaching in the school in Hannibal. The sisters and Johanna's baby would survive together.

In 1861, Johanna married for a second time. Her second husband was John Tobin. John was also an Irish immigrant. He was from the town of Fermoy in County Cork. He was a widower with one daughter named Catherine Bridget. The new family lived in Hannibal. John worked for the local gas company. Johanna gave birth to five more children during her marriage. These were Daniel, Margaret, William, Helen and Michael.

Just like Johanna, John was committed to issues of social justice. Some people said that he was an associate of the abolitionist, John Brown. All of the children in the family were brought up to disavow discrimination of any kind. Johanna and John were also firm believers in education for all of their children. The children attended the school where their Aunt Mary taught. They attended the Catholic Church regularly. Johanna became very influential in the church. She was well respected by the other church members. When her baby Michael died, Johanna turned to her church family for support. The Tobin family was not well off financially. The house the family lived in was small and crowded. The lower level of the house was used as a stable for the family cow and chickens at nighttime.

After Johanna's daughter Mary Ann married, she and her husband, Jack Landrigan, moved to Leadville, Colorado. Miners were pouring into Leadville in hopes of finding gold. Johanna's son Daniel went to live in Leadville as well. Daniel sent money for his two sisters, Margaret and Helen, to visit him in Leadville. Margaret decided to stay and settle in Leadville. She worked in a department store. She met a mining engineer named James Joseph Brown. He was known as J.J. Margaret and J.J were married in 1886. Margaret suggested that her parents and two younger siblings should all move to Leadville to live with them.

J.J owned shares in the Little Johnny Mine which was owned by the Ibex Mining Company. A significant vein of gold was discovered in the mine in 1894. The Browns were suddenly very wealthy. Margaret and J.J decided to move with their two children to the growing city of Denver, Colorado. They bought a mansion on what was known as Capitol Hill. Margaret again invited her parents to move with them to Denver. Johanna and John agreed. John Tobin lived in Denver until he passed away in 1899. Johanna lived with Margaret and J.J.'s family until the end of her days.

Margaret went on to become internationally famous as the 'unsinkable Mrs. Brown' due to her rescue when the ship, the *Titanic* sank in 1912. Other passengers in the lifeboat with Margaret spoke of how she encouraged them. She comforted and cared for the surviving women and children after they had been lifted out of the ocean and onto the ship *Carpathia*. Margaret continued to show concern for others in all walks of life: miners, laborers, women wage earners and those advocating for women's suffrage. Margaret had learned well from her mother Johanna about helping to bring equality into the lives of all she met.

Johanna was afflicted with severe arthritis in her later years. She was bedridden except for Sundays. On Sundays, Johanna managed to stand erect and walk purposefully into the church for Mass. Johanna quietly passed away at home, sitting on Margaret's front porch, gazing at the Rocky Mountains, on April 10, 1905. She had led her children by example and now her work was done.

MONTANA:
Women Helping Women

Ellen Mulkerin Tracy

Ellen Mulkerin was born in Claddaghduff, County Galway, Ireland on February 19, 1880. Claddaghduff was a townland on the western shore of Ireland in the province of Connaught. The land was rugged. Most of the landholders in Claddaghduff were farmers. In 1901, there were 120 people living in the townland. Ellen lived with her parents, Michael and Margaret Lacey Mulkerin in a small house of two to four rooms covered by a thatched roof. Two of Ellen's brothers also lived in the house. Ellen's two sisters, Nora and Margaret immigrated to America.

When Ellen was twenty-one years old, in 1901, she was encouraged to emigrate from Ireland by her two sisters. Once upon a time, the idea of a young woman immigrating on her own would not have been considered proper or wise. Single young Irish men had not been hampered by this convention. In the latter decades of the 19th century, there were not many opportunities for employment for single Irish women in Ireland unless they moved to larger towns where they might find work in domestic services. Even there, competition for these positions was fierce. This led many young women to consider emigrating from Ireland. Ellen was one of the more than 600,000 Irish women under the age of thirty-five years who immigrated to the United States between the years 1885-1920. Most of these women had heard from relatives who had immigrated earlier to America that there were many opportunities for making a good living.

After Ellen arrived in the United States, she made her way to Pittsburgh where her sister Margaret was living. She then headed west to the town of Anaconda in Montana because her sister Nora was living there. The Anaconda Copper Mining Company employed hundreds of Irish workers in the Butte, Montana mines and in their smelting works. There were a number of auxiliary employment opportunities in the town for young single women. There were positions in restaurants, hotels, boarding houses, laundries and in domestic service. Ellen's first job was in the Gavin House, a boarding house on East Park Street.

"The famous Anaconda copper smelters and mines, Butte, Montana
Creator: Standard Scenic Company Published Meadville, PA c 1907
Library of Congress Prints and Photographs Division LC-DIG-stereo-1s13682

Ellen met Timothy Tracy while she was working in the boardinghouse.
Timothy had emigrated from Ballinacourty, County Waterford,
Ireland in 1898. Tim was employed in the smelting works. In 1906,
Ellen and Tim married. They became the parents of eight children.
Additionally, Ellen took seven of her cousins, nieces and nephews
into their home to care for them. The pay Tim earned working in
the smelter did not always provide for this large family, but Ellen
was very good at budgeting and managing the money they had. She
also found other ways to earn money to add to the family coffers.

Ellen's generosity to others was well known in Anaconda. Like the
other women in town, Ellen knew the mining industry could support
a family or send them into decline, depending on market demands, or,
as commonly happened, when injury or death claimed the wage earner
in the mines. The women always rallied around any woman or a family
in distress. Women prepared food, made visitations and helped care for
the children when disaster struck. Ellen's daughter, Isabel, remarked
that her mother "could never say no" when it came to taking people
into their home. "It seemed like we always had such a big family there."

Ellen's daughter, Margaret, stated that their mother had "a penchant for feeding the hungry. If anybody came by she had to feed them."

In 1911, Ellen and Tim became United States citizens. Tim joined the Ancient Order of Hibernians and the Knights of Columbus. He was a member of the Union of Smelters. Ellen became a member of the Daughters of Erin along with other women in town. The family attended St. Peter's Catholic Church. The civic organizations and the church hosted various entertainments for the residents of Anaconda and also held fundraisers for various worthy causes. These organizations provided a support network for the people of the town, especially the women, who spent long hours every day caring for their children, spouse and other family members.

Ellen insisted her children receive a good education. Most of the immigrants who came to work in the mines and smelters, the boarding houses, restaurants and laundries, did not want their children to labor as they did. They saw education as the means for their children to have different, and in their eyes, better lives. Many young women were able to train as teachers. Teachers were held in high regard and earned a living wage. Most of these young women were able to work until they married. After marrying, a woman was expected to leave the paid workforce to concentrate solely on her family's welfare.

Ellen and Tim saw their children grow to adulthood. Most of their children married and began their own families. Many of Ellen and Tim's descendants remained in Anaconda. Others migrated to distant towns. All of them returned to Anaconda when they learned of Ellen's passing on March 8, 1943. Her son William, serving in the U.S. Army in Alaska, was able to fly home at the last moment to attend his mother's funeral. Ellen's humble beginnings under a thatched roof in Ireland did not limit her imagining a different life in America. Her own determination and the support of other women living in similar circumstances nurtured her vision and laid a strong foundation for that vision to flourish.

NEBRASKA:

The Homestead

Mary Walsh Gallagher

In the 1850s, Irish immigrants trying to survive the potato famine immigrated by the thousands to North America. The East Coast cities of New York and Boston, in particular, were severely overcrowded. Newspapers like the *Irish-American Weekly*, printed articles which described favorably the land in the western region of the United States. Places like the Nebraska Territory were opening up for settlement. Three events encouraged many Irish immigrants to consider moving to Nebraska. The Homestead Act was enacted by the U.S. Congress in 1862. Nebraska became a state in 1867. The Transcontinental Railroad was completed in 1868. The railroad made traveling from the East Coast to Nebraska much easier than it had been previously.

The Homestead Act allowed prospective land owners to apply for tracts of government owned land which had been surveyed. Both citizens and immigrants intending to become citizens of the United States could apply for 160 acres of unclaimed land as long as they paid a nominal registration fee. The claimants also had to attest that they had never borne arms against the United States. Once the land was registered, the homesteader had to live on the land for five years and make improvements to the land. Improvements included clearing the land and turning it to farming or ranching, building houses, barns and sheds, or cultivating crops. If those conditions were met, the homesteader could own the land free and clear. Claimants could also own the land before the five years were up if they paid the government $1.25 per acre for the land. After the U.S. Civil War ended, many Union soldiers became homesteaders. They were allowed to deduct their time served from the five year requirement.

Patrick and Mary Gallagher decided to apply for a tract of land under the Homestead Act. They had been living in Luzerne County, Pennsylvania since arriving from Ireland. Patrick was working in the coal mines in Luzerne. Mary Walsh Gallagher, born on February 19, 1846, had given birth to their first child, Hannah, in 1864. Following Hannah, Michael was born in 1866 and John was born in 1867.

Patrick became a naturalized U.S citizen that same year. Patrick and Mary firmed up their plan to migrate west. They first moved to Cass Township, Wapello County, Iowa. Patrick found work in the coal mines there. He planned to save the money the family would need for their next move. Mary gave birth to two more children during their time in Iowa. Elizabeth was born in 1870 and James was born in 1873.

Patrick and Mary saw the advertisements for good farmland in Nebraska. The advertisements claimed, "Rich Farming Lands! For Sale Very Cheap by the Union Pacific Railroad Company. Now is the time to secure a Home in the Great Central Belt Of Population and Wealth and on the line of the World's Highway!" The Gallaghers were ready to stake their claim. In May 1875, they arrived in Nebraska. Patrick chose 160 acres in Niobrara, Nebraska in the "North East Quadrant, Section 7, Township 29, Range 11 West". He paid the registration fee of $14 in order to have his name attached to the claim.

Mary Gallagher Homestead Ownership Record U.S. Homestead Records(NE) 1862-1908,
Gallagher, Mary(1414) U.S. National Archives catalog ID 849143
"Land Entry Records for Nebraska" compiled 1857-1908

Now that the family had their claim, they began the hard work of improving the land. The three older children helped their father even though they were only eleven, nine and seven years old. Mary minded the two younger children while keeping up with household chores. She was expecting another baby during the early days of their claim. She gave birth to a son, Patrick, the following year in 1876. Tragedy struck Mary and the children in January 1877. Patrick died suddenly. Mary and the children were on their own now.

In 1875, married women were not usually property owners. Husbands held property in their names, as well as income, assets and homestead claims. Married women could not take out a claim in their own name when the husband was listed as the head of the house. There was not a prohibition on unmarried women registering a claim for land. Single, widowed or divorced women could claim 160 acres of government land if they followed all of the rules of the Homestead Act. So Mary Gallagher, now a widow, was entitled to hold on to the claim Patrick had registered. Because she was a widow, Mary had two options. She could quit the claim or she could stay on the land with her children. She would still have to make improvements until the five years of the contract were up.

Mary decided to stay on the land. She and the children continued to make improvements. They persevered even though they were plagued with locusts destroying their crops at times. The five year term ended in May 1880. Mary returned to the land office to make her official claim for free and clear ownership of the land. The improvements she listed included four structures built: a house, a stable, a corral and a chicken house. A well had been dug. 2,000 trees had been planted. 35 acres were planted in wheat, oats, barley, corn, rye, potatoes and vegetables. Mary's application was approved on September 6, 1880. She was issued a "Patent for the Tract of Land above described" by the Register of Deeds at the land office in Niobrara, Nebraska.

Mary's two oldest sons were already listed as farmers on the 1880 census when they were fourteen and twelve years old. All of the children worked hard to keep their farm prospering. Mary Gallagher lived nine more years on her land before she passed away on May 27, 1889. She was forty-three years old. The inscription on her headstone summed up her life of hard work and perseverance. "With life's burdens for a pillow, she sank into a dreamless sleep and perfect rest".

NEVADA:

Great in Prosperity, Greater in Adversity

Jessie Callahan Mahoney

Jessie Callahan was born in Austin, Nevada on May 17, 1887. Her father, Dan Callahan, born in 1823, was an Irish immigrant from County Kerry, Ireland. He first came to Nevada as a gold and silver prospector in 1862. His mining stake on a nearby mountain slope gave him a view of the verdant canyon below. Instead of holding onto his mining stake, he took out a claim for a homestead in the canyon. Jessie's mother, Eliza Farrell, born on October 27, 1848, was the daughter of Irish immigrants. Eliza's mother was expecting her during the voyage on the ship from Ireland. Eliza was born in Buenos Aires, Argentina shortly after the ship landed there. Eliza's parents and Eliza did not remain in Buenos Aires. The family continued their journey until they came to San Francisco, California where Eliza grew up. Some years later, during a visit to the California State Fair, held in the town of Sacramento, Eliza met the rancher Dan Callahan. They were married in 1873. By this time, the mountain near Dan's ranch was known as Mount Callahan. The canyon where his ranch was located became known as Callahan Canyon.

Tragedy struck the Callahan family in August 1887 when Jessie was only three months old. Her father had taken a load of potatoes to sell in the town of Austin. On his way home to the ranch in Grass Lake, Dan fell from the seat of his wagon. The fall broke his neck as well as two of his ribs. He died instantly. His death left Eliza and their four children on their own. Fortunately, two of Eliza's older brothers came to her rescue. They loaned Eliza the money to pay off the remaining fees owed on the ranch. The indigenous people living near the ranch were very helpful to Eliza as well. Eliza was determined to keep the ranch. She sold beef, grain, pork and vegetables to the Cortez Mine community. Two years later, Eliza married Hugh McAfee, another rancher.

Jessie was able to obtain a good education from the teachers in schools in Austin, Nevada and in Salt Lake City, Utah. When she was finished with her formal education, she began teaching in a school near the family home. When she was twenty-nine years old, in 1915, she married a man named William Mahoney. William was also an Irish immigrant. He had emigrated from County Cork, Ireland. William had worked at various jobs until he was named the superintendent of the ranch estates owned by William Dunphy. The Dunphy property encompassed over 100,000 acres of land. The Dunphy Ranches utilized 23 different brands for their 8,000 head of cattle. Jessie and William went to live at one of the Dunphy properties known as White House Ranch in the town of Dunphy. One of Jessie's wedding presents was a riding saddle of her own. She loved riding horses and being outside in the open air.

Jessie now managed a huge house. She and some of the indigenous women who lived at the ranch took care of the housekeeping. Jessie was in charge of the cooks who kept the many ranch hands fed every day. She was also expected to host the many visitors who came to the ranch. Among the visitors were other ranchers and buyers of cattle, as well as visitors and relatives passing through the area. Dignitaries, politicians and clergy also came to visit. The most prominent visitors were members of the Dunphy family who periodically traveled from San Francisco to check on the state of their ranches.

Jessie gave birth to four children during these years. Usually, she traveled to San Francisco for the births, then spent some time recovering before traveling back home to Nevada. She was a devoted mother. Her children thought highly of her. One of her daughters, Aileen, said of Jessie, "Wherever my mother was, was a lovely place to be. No matter what she was doing, she put magic in it; my father too..they were the type of people who come into the room and lights and music go on."

Jessie felt strongly that her children should receive formal education. She encouraged all of the children to read widely. She made sure that there were always books and newspapers to read in their home. After more than twenty years managing the many Dunphy properties, the properties were split among different owners. William no longer had a position on the estates. He and Jessie bought their own ranch near the town of Beowawe, Eureka County, Nevada. They bought their own cattle and designed their own brand. Two of their children, Dan and Theresa, joined them in managing the ranch.

Both William and Jessie took an interest in local politics. William was elected to the Eureka County Commission. He served until 1945 when he passed away. Jessie was appointed by the governor of Nevada to fulfill the remainder of Wiliam's term of office. She did this admirably, and so, was then elected a commissioner, serving for two terms.

William's death did not cause the family to lose their ranch. Jessie, Dan and Theresa continued to operate the ranch. Another daughter, Mary, lived at home while teaching in a school in the town of Beowawe. Jessie's

eldest daughter Aileen and her husband lived nearby. Aileen was also teaching in a school. Aileen said, "Jessie had always wanted a ranch of her own, instead of managing someone else's property. She especially loved the ranch at Beowawe, with its wide open views. She took a knowledgeable interest in every aspect of the ranch and cattle operation and was a very shrewd rancher."

Dan Mahoney was killed in an automobile accident in 1952. After his death, Jessie and Theresa managed the ranch together. They made improvements to the property and continued its prosperity. Four years later, in 1956, Jessie passed away

"Saddle" Photographer Bailey Alexander 2022
Public Domain through Unsplash

at the age of sixty-nine years. Inscribed on her tombstone were the words that she had lived by throughout her entire life. "Magnus in prosperitate, major in adversitate." "Great in prosperity, greater in adversity."

NEW HAMPSHIRE:

In the Line of Service

Teresa Margaret Murphy

Teresa Margaret Murphy was born on October 31, 1891 in Market Hill, County Armagh, Ireland. Her parents were Thomas and Ellen Heaney Murphy. Teresa was the fourth child of six siblings born into the family. Teresa emigrated from Londonderry, Ireland aboard the ship *Parisian* in 1910 when she was nineteen years old. She attended the New Hampshire State Hospital Training School in Concord, New Hampshire. When Teresa graduated in 1915, she was granted a license to practice nursing in the state of New Hampshire. One year later, she signed a Declaration of Intention, the necessary form for completion before becoming a citizen of the United States. She was working as a nurse and living in Penacook, New Hampshire.

When the U.S. became engaged in World War I, on the side of the Allies, Teresa volunteered her nursing skills. She joined the Red Cross and was sent to England in February 1918. The Red Cross expanded its nursing services to meet the need for nursing personnel to aid the U.S. Army and Navy. During this time, the Red Cross placed 19,931 nurses on active duty. Many of these nurses were sent to Europe. 296 Red Cross nurses lost their lives during their wartime service. The nurses were often close to battle fronts. They were constantly exposed to all of the dangers of wartime. Back at home in Concord, the Concord Friendly Club raised a flag to the four women known to them to be currently serving as nurses overseas.

Teresa may have been originally stationed in Base No. # 3 Hospital, located in Vauclaire, France. The Hospital served men primarily affected by pulmonary tuberculosis. The hospital site was then moved to London, England. Pulmonary tuberculosis was infectious. All of those working with the infected were susceptible to infection as well. Teresa spent many hours every day in the hospital attending to the patients with pulmonary tuberculosis. Sadly, she too became infected. On November 9, 1918, Teresa passed away from tuberculosis. She was twenty-seven years old. The date was only two days before Armistice was declared on November 11, 1918. At the time of her death, the doctors and nurses in the hospital in England were treating nearly 3,000 ill and wounded patients.

Teresa's next of kin was her paternal uncle, Owen Murphy, who lived in Cumberland, Rhode Island. He received the official military telegram informing him of Teresa's death. Teresa's name was listed on a memorial plaque as one of the alumni of the New Hampshire School of Nursing who served during World War I. The American Legion Post in Penacook, New Hampshire also listed her on their World War I Memorial dedicated to those who lost their lives in the war.

Teresa's grave is located in the Brookwood American Military Cemetery in Brookwood, Woking Borough, Surrey, England. In 1919, the families of the U.S. Americans killed during the war were given the option of bringing their family member back to a cemetery of their choice in the United States or leaving them among comrades in an American cemetery in Europe. Teresa's surviving family members decided that she would remain in Europe. Teresa's life was not long in years, yet this Irish immigrant portrayed loyalty, compassion, professionalism and heroism which is admired still today.

"New Hampshire World War I Red Cross Nurses Memorial Plaque"
Courtesy of the New Hampshire Historical Society

The Red Cross Nurses

"Out where the line of battle cleaves
The horizon of woe
And sightless warriors clutch the leaves
The Red Cross nurses go.
In where the cots of agony
Mark death's unmeasured tide-
Bear up the battle's harvesters-
The Red Cross nurses glide.
Look! Where the hell of steel has torn
Its way through slumbering earth
The orphaned urchins kneel forlorn
And wonder at their birth.
Until, above them, calm and wise
With smile and guiding hand,
God looking through their gentle eyes,
The Red Cross nurses stand."

Thomas L. Masson

NEW JERSEY:
Doctor Kelly Makes House Calls

Gertrude Bride Kelly

"Dr. Gertrude Bride Kelly"
The New York Times, February 17, 1934

Brigid Kelly was born on February 10, 1862 in Carrick-on-Suir, County Tipperary, Ireland. She was one of nine siblings born to Jeremiah and Kate Forrest Kelly. She was also known as Gertrude B. Kelly. Among friends, she was known as Bride. Bride and her family immigrated to the United States in 1868. Hoboken, New Jersey became their new home. Jeremiah Kelly was a teacher. Eventually, he became a school principal in one of New Jersey's public schools.

Bride's parents were members of the New Jersey Land League. This organization was founded in solidarity with the Irish Land League active in Ireland during this time. The Irish Land League sought to have untenable rents lowered for Irish tenant farmers. The League also fought for tenant farmers to have the assurance of fixity of rent from their landlords. The League's biggest goal was to have the tenant farmer's land to become owned by the tenant. This would allow the owners of the land to sell the land if they wished. In New Jersey, the primary purpose of the American version of the Land League was to provide financial support for their counterpart in Ireland.

104

Bride attended public schools through her graduation from high school. After graduation, Bride also began teaching in New Jersey public schools. She had another ambition which was to study medicine. She was accepted into the Women's Medical College of the New York Infirmary for Women and Children. Her goal was to become a doctor. Bride obtained her medical degree, which qualified her as a surgeon, at the age of twenty-two years, in 1888.

Bride was concerned about, and primarily worked with, women and children living in tenement housing on the Lower East Side of Manhattan and in Newark, New Jersey. She established a medical clinic in the Chelsea neighborhood of Manhattan. In neighborhoods often referred to as slums, Bride saw the people who needed her medical skills the most.

Bride was known as a political activist for women and children and for the cause of Irish nationalism. There were those who found her views objectionable. She refused to consider women sex workers as 'fallen women'. Instead, she regarded them as 'economic victims'. She defended this view in an article she wrote for the magazine *Liberty*. She stated, "Women choose the sex worker profession because they could not make an adequate living through respectable forms of labor. We find all sorts of schemes for making men moral and women religious, but no scheme which proposes to give woman the fruits of her labor." In a time when women who supported the feminist movement were derided for their views, Bride wrote, "The woman's cause is man's-they rise or sink/Together,-dwarfed or god-like bond or free." She believed in "universal liberty, equality of rights, individual responsibility..as the moving principles of societary progress."

Bride donated money to the cause of Irish nationalism. She donated money to the Irish Republicans who carried out the 1916 Easter Rising for Ireland's independence. She also sent money to the Irish families who witnessed fathers, sons and brothers in the volunteer Irish Army imprisoned after the Rising. Bride's support of Ireland self-rule led her and others to instigate a blockade of the British embassy in Washington D.C. The group assembled in Chelsea at one of the piers. Bride and the other women assembled carried signs stating, "There Can Be No Peace While British Militarism Rules the World". Many Irish longshoremen joined the strike. Other immigrant workers also joined. News of the blockade spread from Chelsea to Brooklyn and then to New Jersey and Boston.

Bride did not claim any religious affiliation. She described herself as an 'unredeemed pagan'. Her generosity to those less fortunate was legendary and without direction from any organized religious group. She was known to waive the fees for her patients, especially those living in the tenements. More often, those she had helped would find a $5 bill underneath the plate upon which the family had shared their meager meal with her.

When Bride was in her late sixties, she was seriously injured in an automobile accident. Her injuries left her an invalid. To honor her many years of service, and in grateful appreciation, over 500 people attended a reception in Bride's honor which was held in the Hotel McAlpin, in New York City. Medical colleagues, social workers, fair labor and union members, members of clergy, city leaders and friends all came together to say 'thank-you' to a woman who had done so much for so many. Some members of Ireland's government attended as well.

On February 24, 1934, Bride passed away. She had not married, nor had she children. Her longtime partner, Mary Walsh, survived her. As a final tribute to her, New York mayor Fiorello LaGuardia commissioned a playground in the Chelsea neighborhood of New York City to be named for Bride Kelly. The playground stands today, a testimony to a woman who embraced every cause to uplift people of any age to a life of dignity, equality and access to opportunities and health care for better lives.

NEW MEXICO:

Doctor Sister Mary

Sister Mary de Sales Elizabeth Leheny

"Sister Mary de Sales" Courtesy of the Sisters of Charity of Cincinnati Archives, rights retained

In 1865, the first Sisters of Charity, a religious organization of women dedicated to the education of poor children and the care of those who were injured or ill or orphaned, arrived in Santa Fe, in the New Mexico Territory. They were answering a call from the Catholic Bishop, Father John Lamy, who insisted that all persons in the Territory, regardless of ethnicity, social standing, ability to pay or religion be given an opportunity for education and compassionate health care. Four women journeyed from the Motherhouse in Cincinnati, Ohio to answer this call. The Sisters took in orphans and turned their domicile into St. Vincent's Hospital. They were followed by four more women in 1867. The Sisters did not live in extravagant surroundings. "The kitchen had a mud floor and a mud roof, with a zinc patch above the stove to keep out the rain." Water for laundry and daily needs was carried in buckets from a spring located in a nearby pasture. Sixteen years later, in 1881, three more Sisters traveled by train and carriage to Santa Fe as the number of people the Sisters served continued to grow. One of the new Sisters who arrived was Sister Mary de Sales.

Sister Mary de Sales Leheny was born in 1856 in Cincinnati, Ohio. Her parents gave her the name Elizabeth. She was the eldest daughter of Thomas Leheny, born in Ireland in 1823 to Owen and Elizabeth Callaghan Leheny and Maria Byrne Leheny, the daughter of Malachi and Ann Byrne from County Wicklow, Ireland. Thomas and Marie married in Cincinnati on October 29, 1854. Seven more children after Elizabeth were eventually born into the family. Elizabeth attended school until the age of thirteen or fourteen. After she left school, she worked in a shoe factory in order to help with the family finances. In 1880, Elizabeth joined the novitiate of the Sisters of Charity in Cincinnati. She took on a new name when she professed her vows. She was now known as Sister Mary de Sales. The following year, she was assigned to the mission in Santa Fe.

The long, low-ceiling adobe building the Sisters ran as St. Vincent's Orphanage also served as one of the few school buildings in the Territory. The Sisters did not have supplies or furniture, other than rough benches for the pupils. There were only two textbooks. The Sister teaching the class used one of the books. All of the students shared the other book. The number of orphans continued to grow as parents were killed in mining accidents or by diseases. Eventually, the Sisters accepted students who came from private homes. The Santa Fe School Board charged tuition for these students. The fee was meant to pay the teacher's salary. The Sisters did not accept salaries. Instead, they used the money to buy supplies for the students and classroom. Four months after Sister Mary arrived in Santa Fe, there were 35 orphans living with the Sisters at St. Vincent's. Five years later, the number had doubled. Bishop Lamy wanted a trade school building erected that would better serve the children. In particular, he wanted girls to learn practical trades and skills so they would be able to take care of themselves after leaving the Sisters.

The Sisters were also always in need of funds for the care of their patients. The Territorial Legislature passed a measure which allocated $100 per month for the hospital for patient care. To show their gratitude, the Sisters helped the orphan children put on a program for the legislative body. One of the senators was so impressed, he gave a further donation of $100 so that the Sisters could purchase a piano.

When the building meant to be the trade school was completed, the plans changed. The building was immediately put to use as the new St. Vincent's Hospital. The number of sick or dying patients had grown so quickly, there was not enough room to house them all in the Sisters' quarters. Although there were no specially trained nurses working in the hospital, Sister Mary and other Sisters did what they could to provide relief and compassionate care. The women often worked around the clock for many days and nights in succession. Sister Mary worked with the same surgeon at the hospital, Dr. James A. Massive for twenty years. She was his First Assistant and received her medical training from him.

There was not an operating theater for surgery. "Operations were performed in the patients' rooms. The operating table was one from the doctor's office or a folding table which could be set up for the operation. Two boilers of water, one prepared the previous day, the other on the morning of the operation were used in sterilizing the instruments." Dr. Massive and the other doctors showed Sister Mary how to make sponges used in surgical procedures. Sister Mary treated the miners who were brought to the hospital after explosions in the mines. Those not killed by the blasts often had stones embedded in their eyes, faces, hands and arms. Oftentimes, Sister Mary had only basic tools to help her remove the stones. She saved one man using only a forceps and a pen knife.

Many of the patients whose injuries or illnesses proved beyond the capabilities of Sister Mary and the doctors were destitute and without any family to claim their bodies. During post mortem examinations, Sister Mary learned much. She used this knowledge with future patients when they presented with similar symptoms. In spite of successfully treating many of the injured, many patients still died. "The Sisters had plain board coffins made in dozen lots; these were stained as they were needed." The number of people who did recover from their maladies grew over time. The trade school building was officially turned over to the Sisters running St. Vincent's Hospital in 1883. Sister Mary and the other nursing Sisters were delighted. The building boasted steam heat and became the first sanatorium in the entire region.

People began to learn of the health benefits the dry, warm climate of New Mexico offered. People from the East Coast cities began to come to Santa Fe to recover from respiratory illnesses. Only two years after the Sisters had moved into the new St. Vincent's Sanatorium, another building was constructed to house those who came to Santa Fe for treatments. This building was even larger which allowed the Sisters to take in more patients. It was not always possible for a person to make their way into the town where the sanatorium was located. Sister Mary often found herself, in company with another Sister, heading out in the night to somewhere miles distant to tend to an injured or suffering person needing care. Sometimes, she traveled to a mining camp to help an injured person. Once, she was called to the town of Santa Cruz where a priest was dying. Sister Mary and another Sister made the journey and tended to the priest. After two weeks, the priest was well enough to make the journey to the hospital in Santa Fe. "Proper care and treatment restored his health," Sister Mary said.

In 1896, a fire destroyed most of the hospital. While some of the Sisters made sure all of the children in the vicinity were safe, Sister Mary and the other nursing Sisters transported patients to safety. Sister Mary carried those who could not walk upon her back. She was never again able to stand straight after these acts of selflessness.

After twenty years of service in Santa Fe, Sister Mary received a great honor. The medical board of New Mexico conferred upon her the Degree of Doctor of Medicine, license number 217, February 21, 1901. Her degree was signed by all of the members of the New Mexico Territory Medical Board. She was the first woman in New Mexico to be officially recognized as a medical doctor. Her years of training next to surgeons and her willingness to continue learning, while also providing compassionate care, superseded formal medical training which had only recently become available to women in the United States. Her own sister, Anna Leheny, sixteen years younger than Sister Mary, was present when the medical degree was handed to her sister. Anna had joined the religious order as well. She was known as Sister Mary Seraphina Leheny. The two sisters lived together in Santa Fe.

Sister Mary de Sales served the people of Santa Fe as a medical professional and as a Sister of Charity for over fifty years. When she was recognized for her years of service with the Sisters of Charity, a local newspaper reporter remarking on the event wrote, "She is indeed one of the leading living authorities on Santa Fe of the early days and is regarded by many as one of the best informed persons in the state on the two very vital subjects-life and death."

It was not an illness like tuberculosis that led to Sister Mary's death in her seventy-ninth year. Instead, characteristically, she died while carrying out a service of compassion towards one of her patients. A man was in the hospital, nearing death, but without family or friends. Sister Mary stopped to see him after her night shift. When she asked the man if she could bring him anything, he answered, "Sister, I'd like a bracer of good strong coffee." Sister Mary went to get the coffee which was in the kitchen of another building. The night was cold and the footpath to the other building was icy. Sister Mary slipped on the ice. She could not stand up again. She lay, one hip broken, helpless until she was found some time later. She lingered for two weeks in the sanatorium before passing away on November 29, 1934, at the age of seventy eight years. The good doctor had served her patients well.

NEW YORK:

"Don't Iron While the Strike is Hot"

Kate Mullany Fogarty

North of Albany, New York, the city of Troy lies on the east side of the Hudson River. The Mohawk River, a tributary of the Hudson River, joins the Hudson north of Troy. The location of the city near the rivers' confluence made it an excellent site for industrial development in the early 19th century. Sufficient water was available for generating power in the many manufacturing and service facilities that employed thousands of people who found work and settled in Troy.

Both men and women found work in Troy. While men comprised most of the workforce, working as ironmongers and molders, bricklayers, printers and plumbers, many women worked in textile mills, working with cotton and looms. The biggest employer of women, however, was in laundry services. More than 50% of the women working outside the home were employed as washers, starchers and ironers in commercial laundries. In the mid 1800s, there were fourteen commercial laundries in Troy. By the beginning of the 20th century, Troy was known as the 'Collar City' due to there being over twenty laundries taking in shirtfronts, detachable collars and cuffs. Many of these women were unmarried and living at home with other family members. They used their earnings to ease the financial struggles of their parents. Most of the women working the grueling 12-14 hour days were immigrants.

Catherine Mullany, known as Kate, worked in a laundry. She was born around the year 1845 in Sligo, Ireland. Kate had emigrated from Ireland with her parents, Dominic and Bridget Mullany, and her older sister Mary, during the famine year of 1850. The Mullanys settled in Troy. Three other children were born during the next ten years. Dominic passed away in 1861. His death left the family without any income. Kate's mother was often unwell and not fit to work outside the family home. It fell to Kate to go to work in one of the laundries in order to provide for the family. Kate's older sister Mary managed the housework and helped care for the younger siblings.

"Folding and ironing linen collars, Troy, NY"
Library of Congress Prints and Photographs Division LC-USZ62-99898

Working in a commercial laundry was not without danger. The women's hands were constantly immersed in boiling hot water. Caustic chemicals, such as bleach, were added during the cleaning process. Initially, the starching of collars was done by hand. When starching machines took over this part of the process, many women suffered severe burns from them. The hot irons used to press the collars were another source of burns. Collar workers accepted the perils of their work because their pay was higher than what was paid to women working in other service sector jobs.

Still, Kate realized that working conditions for women in the collar laundries could and should be improved. When she was nineteen years old, she and another worker, Esther Keegan, began discussing the idea of a union for the collar workers. They took their lead from the men who had recently formed and joined the Iron Molder's Union. This Union had been able to achieve better working conditions for its members. There was also a Cigar Maker's Union and a Printer's Union. Kate felt that it was time for a Collar Laundry Union. Kate and Esther were not daunted by the fact that there were not any unions for women industrial workers. They were not put off knowing that there was enormous competition for collar laundry jobs. They believed strongly that women working in industries deserved a fair wage, safe working conditions and reasonable work shifts.

Not only was it difficult to imagine starting a union, it was difficult to find the time or a place to hold discussions with the other women working in laundries. Somehow, Kate and Ester were able to devise ways to talk with the other women. They found many of them receptive to their idea of forming a union. On February 23, 1864, at 12:00 noon, 300 women from fourteen commercial laundries walked off their jobs. The Collar Laundry Union workers were on strike. Kate had helped design a banner which the women carried. The Collar Laundry Union motto was, "Don't Iron While the Strike is Hot".

Kate and the other women on strike demanded a 20-25% raise in pay. Additionally, they wanted the owners of the laundries to do something about the dangerous heat of the starching machines. The laundry owners told the strikers that they could not afford to pay them more for their work because they would have to pass that increase onto the collar manufacturers. The situation was at an impasse. For five days, Kate, Esther and the other women stayed away from their jobs. Finally, on February 28, 1864, some of the laundry owners gave in to the striking workers' demands. The other laundry owners followed. The first strike by the first female union was a success!

The Collar Laundry Union stayed strong and active for the next five years. In 1866, the Union contributed $1,000 to the Iron Molders Union when they were on strike. This was important because it demonstrated that the women's union would support causes brought up by typically men's unions. When the contribution became publicly known, the Troy Trades Assembly invited the Collar Laundry Union to join their affiliation. The women unionists were now acknowledged as other union workers first, and women second.

A second strike by the Collar Laundry Union in 1866 won for the workers an increase in pay from $8 per week to $14 per week. Kate offered to share the expertise that she and the other Collar Union leaders had amassed with other women trade workers who were planning to unionize. One of the groups that took advantage of this offer was the fledgling Ironers Union. Kate assisted them in a strike in 1868 which successfully led to the workers receiving a pay increase.

Two months later, in September 1868, Kate was invited to attend the National Labor Congress held in New York City. On the last day of the Congress, William Sylvia, the president of the National Labor Union, appointed Kate as assistant secretary of the Union. This was the first time that a woman held an official administrative position in the Union. Kate corresponded with other women industrial workers in order to facilitate more women's unions across the country.

Kate and other Collar Laundry Unionists supported strikes for better pay and better working conditions for both men and women in all trades and industries. She assisted when the women starchers struck for higher wages and rejoiced with them when their demands were met.

In 1869, Kate had saved enough money so that she could buy a house for her family. The double house was three stories in height, and made of bricks. She was proud of this accomplishment and happy to see her family living in better conditions. In the same year, the Collar Laundry Union again struck for higher wages for the women. This time, however, the results did not go in the Union's favor. The laundry owners and the collar manufacturers teamed up against the Union. The collar manufacturers refused to send collars and cuffs to any laundry that employed union workers. The laundry owners hired non-union replacement workers.

Kate and the other leaders of the Collar Laundry Union decided to set up a type of cooperative laundry with collars and cuffs brought in from out of town manufacturers. The laundry owners and Troy manufacturers found a way to prevent the out of town manufacturers from selling their products in Troy. Still, the Collar Laundry Union leaders did not give up. They decided to form the Union Line Collar and Cuff Manufactory. They would make their own collars and cuffs for sale. Kate was elected the first president of the company. The new company was able to secure a sizable contract from Mr. A.T. Steward, a man known as the 'merchant prince of New York', when he agreed to buy their collars and cuffs. The new union owned company now had a chance to make a success of themselves.

Alas, it was not to be. The collar manufacturers thwarted the company's plans by introducing something new: a cellulloid collar. The Union Line Collar and Cuff Manufactory could not compete with these new collars. Their company collapsed. The following year, the Collar Laundry Union was dissolved. All of the union members had to return to work at former wages. Kate did remain a member of the Starchers Union. She remained active in the labor movement, continuing to support the idea of workers' cooperatives.

In the year 1870, Kate married a man named John Fogarty. She and John first lived in the house Kate had purchased. They moved to their own home in 1875 and remained there for five years. After John passed away in 1900, Kate returned once again to her home at 350 Eighth Street in Troy. Kate passed away in 1906. Her contributions to the women's labor movement and to all workers' labor movements provided successive numbers of workers with ideas and organizational methods to aid in their own struggles for fair pay, safe working conditions and the respect and dignity they deserved.

NORTH CAROLINA:

Lost and Found

Sister Annie Colclough

The idea of education for all women in Ireland or the United States was not generally accepted in the early 19th century. Many families, communities and governing leaders did not see a need for equipping girls with formal education. Women were not generally allowed to interact in legal or business matters on their own behalf. The decisions they made after marrying concerned their children, raising them and keeping house. Some girls were taught basic reading, writing and simple sums but that was the extent of their formal education. However, a change from this viewpoint was on the horizon and moving slowly forward.

The Order of Religious Education was founded in 1817 in Normandy, France by a Catholic priest, Father Louis Lafosse and four women. Father Lafosse and the women believed girls should have the opportunity for a solid education. They wanted to establish a school with high academic standards for girls. They also wanted to respect each girl who came to their school as a person in her own right.

Some years later, in 1869, a daughter was born to Thomas and Catherine Reynolds Colclough in Lucan, County Dublin, Ireland. The baby was named Annie Mary Josephine Colclough. Annie came to know about Father Lafosse's school at a very young age. Her mother Catherine was not in good health. When Annie was nine years old, her mother's chronic illness forced the family to make a difficult decision. Catherine would move to France where it was hoped she might regain her health. Annie would accompany her mother to France.

Not long after their arrival, Catherine died. Annie was sent to live with Sisters of the Order of Religious Education. Her mother's older sister was one of the teaching nuns at the school. Annie's older sister had joined the order as well. Leaving Annie at the school and in the Sisters' care gave her a stable home and family around her. She did not return to Ireland again.

When Annie was old enough to discern her own plans for her life, she too decided to join the Order of Religious Education Sisters. She remained in France until government policies forced many religious institutions to close. She was sent to Farnborough, England where she lived for two years.

In December 1906, Annie and three other Sisters sailed from the port at Le Havre, France for New York City. They had been invited to join other Sisters in their Order who lived in West Virginia. Annie was firm in her conviction for this mission. She carried forty dollars with her to pay for herself and the other Sisters to reach their final destination. As it turned out, West Virginia was not to be their final destination.

Almost one year later, in November 1907, Annie and three Sisters arrived in Asheville, North Carolina. Initially, the women were assigned to work in a convalescent home. Instead, the Sisters discussed starting a school for girls in Asheville. They planned to accept students from all religious denominations. The school would take boarding students as well as day students. Among Annie's many duties would be teaching music classes. Twenty-two girls were enrolled in the first class of the Hillside Convent School. The school gained in popularity and the number of students rose quickly. In only a few months, a larger building was needed to house students. The next location found was also soon too small for the number of girls attending.

In 1910, a large three story, eighty room building was acquired by the Sisters. The building had formerly been known as the Victoria Hotel. As the initial group of students grew older, a clamor was raised to see them through higher education. The Sisters expanded their class offerings from elementary level to secondary and then college level courses. The college became known as St. Genevieve-of-the-Pines College. Sister Annie continued teaching music classes through all of the changes over the years.

In 1925, Sister Annie made her declaration to become a citizen of the United States. In the descriptive portion of the application, she described herself as "white, fair complexion, height 4 feet 11 inches, weight 100 pounds, color of hair gray." Her application was approved.

In later years, Annie became known as Mother Annie Colclough. She continued to teach music to St. Genevieve students until ill health forced her to retire after her 70th year. Mother Annie passed away on November 30, 1942. She was buried on December 2, 1942 in the Sisters' cemetery located in Fletcher, North Carolina. In her obituary, Mother Annie was remembered as a woman who "made many friends by her kindness, thoughtfulness, and self-forgetfulness".

Mother Annie's impact on those around her did not end with her life. During her lifetime, she had become well known for finding articles lost by others. This continued even after her death. Fellow Sisters continued to turn to Mother Annie in prayer when they lost something important to them. Other people, not in the Order, learned of this and began offering petitions to Mother Annie when they had lost something. Many people attested that their prayers and petitions were answered. The young Irish immigrant who was lost at her mother's death was found by the Sisters of the Order for Religious Education. She believed, as they did, that young girls and women should be allowed a thorough education so they might find their way through their own lives.

"Sister Annie Colclough and Sister Mary Colclough" Courtesy of Sisters of Religious Education
Mary Colclough (left) and Annie Colclough(right)

NORTH DAKOTA:

In One Lifetime

Sister Anita Margaret M. O'Conor

Throughout the 19th century, the approved roles that women could take on mainly centered around home and family. One group of women chose a different path which led them away from the roles of wife and mother. These were the women who entered religious orders. While devotion to God and their religion were paramount in their decision to enter into religious life, many of these women found themselves working in positions that were not considered the norm for a woman. Sisters, or nuns, were teachers, nurses, physicians, midwives, business women, administrators, social workers, child care workers, disaster relief workers, along with many other job titles. Within their religious orders, the women were able to further their education and were encouraged to take on roles that other women, not in religious orders, were not allowed.

One such woman was Margaret M. O'Connor. Maggie, as she was known during her childhood years, was the daughter of Margaret Murphy and Hugh O'Connor. She was born on July 15, 1865. The family lived in County Cork, Ireland. Maggie immigrated to the United States with three of her brothers. They landed in New York in April 1888. The siblings directly set out for the Dakota Territory. They settled in New Rockford, Dakota Territory. There was prairie land all around. There were no roads or churches or schools. On July 7, 1888, Maggie signed her oath of allegiance to become a United States citizen. On November 2nd of the following year, North Dakota joined the Union simultaneously with South Dakota as the 39th and 40th states.

In 1891, each of the four O'Connor siblings took out a claim in their own names for 160 acres of land as allowed by the Homestead Act of 1862. Maggie was excited to think that in five year's time, as long as she adhered to the stipulations of the Act, she would be the legal owner of her land. Maggie was twenty-five years old when she filed her claim. At that time, less than 10% of homesteaders were women. One year after filing her claim, Maggie entered the novitiate of the Sisters of St. Joseph of Carondelet of St. Paul, Minnesota. She took on a new name, Sister Anita. During

"Margaret O'Connor Declaration of Intent" Courtesy of Sisters of St. Joseph of Carondelet, St. Paul, Minnesota

the next nine years, Sister Anita worked to improve her claim. She had to meet the residency requirements for her claim as well. Minimally, she had to travel from St. Paul to her claim in New Rockford, North Dakota on 'residency day'. This was the one day in the year that homesteaders had to show that they were living on their land. During the other days of the year, Sister Anita was in charge of food services for the Academy of Holy Angels in St. Paul from 1894-1907. The Academy was a boarding and day school for girls from elementary through secondary school.

On March 17, 1900, Sister Anita was granted full ownership of her land. The following year, she sold her land to her brother Timothy. She donated the money from the sale to her religious order. From then on, Sister Anita worked solely in her role as a Sister. In 1907, she moved on from the Academy of Holy Angels to St. Michael's Hospital in Grand Forks, North Dakota. She again supervised all of the food services. In 1913, she moved back to St. Paul where she continued supervising food services in different institutions run by the Sisters. She was known to maintain high standards regarding food preparation and safety. She was strict with the younger Sisters who worked under her tutelage, but softened any words of criticism with "her gentle Irish humor". It was said of her that "she loved to help the poor or indeed anyone who seemed helpless or in great need."

Sister Anita continued in her supervisory capacity well into her eighth decade. Illness forced her finally to desist. She was diagnosed with cancer which, among other infirmities, caused her to lose sight in one eye. She was often in great pain but no one ever heard her complain about her symptoms or her fate. She passed away on December 15, 1956 at the age of ninety-two years. She had been a member of the Sisters for sixty-five years. Sister Anita's entire life had not followed the usual path a woman's life followed. She had been a young immigrant, then a homesteader, then a landowner and then a woman of service. She followed her own path, leading by example and showing that a woman could accomplish much in one lifetime.

OHIO:
Angel of Alcoholics Anonymous

Sister Ignatia Gavin

"Sister Ignatia" Courtesy of the Sisters of Charity of St. Augustine Archives

At the beginning of the new year 1889, a baby girl was born to Patrick and Barbara Neary Gavin in Shanvalley, County Mayo, Ireland. The parents named their baby Bridget Della Gavin. Her older brother Patrick completed the Gavin family. Patrick Gavin was a farmer on a plot of land known as Gavin's Field. Eking out a living for the small family was an arduous task. In the springtime of 1896, The Gavin family, along with other relatives, left Ireland for new lives in the United States. Della was seven years old. The Gavins settled in Cleveland, Ohio.

Patrick found work as a laborer. Della began attending school. Her teachers noticed that she had a gift for music so Della was given extra instruction in music theory and instruments. By the time she graduated from secondary school, Della was giving private music lessons. The money she earned helped to support her family. Della joined the Sisters of Charity of St. Augustine in 1914. She took the name Mary Ignatia after her profession of vows. Eleven years later, Sister Ignatia earned her Bachelor of Music degree from the University of Notre Dame in South Bend, Indiana. She began teaching music at the congregation's school, St. Augustine Academy in Lakewood, Ohio. She remained teaching here for several years. Much as she wished to share her love of music with others, teaching was not a good fit for Sister Ignatia's health. Her superiors reassigned her to the post of registrar at their new St. Thomas Hospital in Akron, Ohio in 1928.

In her new post, keeping track of patients coming into the hospital, Sister Ignatia noticed that many of these people were exhibiting signs of excessive alcohol consumption. She recognized the signs of too much alcohol because she had seen similar symptoms back in Ireland among some of her neighbors. Her mother had always told her to pray for those afflicted by 'the drink'. Drunkenness was thought by most people to be a moral failure on the part of the inebriated person. Often in hospitals, people coming into the emergency room were not treated compassionately if they were thought to be drunk.

One of the interns in the hospital where Sister Ignatia worked was Thomas Scuderi. Instead of scorn, he and Sister Ignatia moved the inebriated patients out of the emergency room and into a room across from the hospital chapel. They allowed these people to sober up before they were sent back out onto the streets. Patients experiencing delirium tremens, or those who were too loud, were given morphine by Thomas Scuderi. The morphine allowed the patients to sleep. When they woke again, Sister Ignatia gave them coffee, followed by fruit juice mixed with Karo syrup. Sister Ignatia listened compassionately to the stories the recovering patients told her. She tried to counsel them away from alcohol. While their methods were illicit, both Thomas Scuderi and Sister Ignatia realized that alcohol addiction required more than willpower to overcome because it was a disease.

In 1934, Sister Ignatia met and developed a friendship with Doctor Robert Smith, a surgeon on the staff. Dr. Bob was a recovering alcoholic who wanted to help other alcoholics live healthier lives without alcohol. He also believed that more than willpower was needed to combat the disease of alcoholism. Dr. Bob worked with a man named Bill Wilson, another recovering alcoholic. The two men devised the Twelve Steps of recovery to combat the disease. Their Steps included admitting one's powerlessness over alcohol, trusting in a higher power, medicine, solo and group counseling, support groups, service to others and prayer. Sister Ignatia joined in with the men's mission. She and Dr. Bob persuaded the hospital administration to dedicate a ward for recovering alcoholics. On August 16, 1935, Sister Ignatia admitted the first patient suffering from alcohol excess to the ward. The patient was admitted with a diagnosis of acute gastritis. This was the first time that a patient was officially medically treated for alcoholism. St. Thomas Hospital was the first hospital in the United States to set up a medical ward for the treatment of alcoholism.

Sister Ignatia was one of the first people to utilize coffee as a sobering aid for these patients. She came up with the idea of giving Sacred Heart Badges to patients at different milestone moments in their recovery. She told her patients the Sacred Heart Badge signified a commitment to God, to the ideals of the newly formed organization, Alcoholics Anonymous and to their recovery. She advised patients as they left the hospital that they had a responsibility to return their badge if they were going to have an alcoholic drink. Many of Sister Ignatia's patients credited the badges with keeping them from taking an alcoholic drink.

Twenty-four years after she began working at St. Thomas's Hospital, Sister Ignatia was transferred to St. Vincent Charity Hospital in Cleveland, Ohio. Her many colleagues, friends and former patients were loath to see her leave Akron and St. Thomas's. Sister Ignatia said to all of these people, "We're just like people in the Army, you know. We go where we are sent...I was there for 24 years... and finally the obedience came that I was to go to Charity and work with A.A there." When she arrived in Cleveland in 1952, Sister Ignatia set about designing and instituting an alcohol treatment wing at this hospital. When one of the hospital board members balked at her plan to include a coffee bar in the new wing, Sister Ignatia said, "Let's forget about it if you're not going to give us the proper setup." She knew that coffee was essential for many of her recovering patients. The coffee bar was built into the new wing. The name of the new wing was Rosary Hall Solarium. The initials, RHS, commemorated Dr. Robert Holbrook Smith, who had passed away in 1950.

Thousands of people received treatment and care at Rosary Hall Solarium. People noticed that Sister Ignatia seemed to be the heart and soul of the place. To facilitate the recovery of patients, "medicine, spiritual nourishment and brotherly love regularly produced miracles of recovery..." Some of the many people treated at the solarium were priests and nuns who suffered from alcohol addiction. Sister Ignatia was instrumental in beginning the Al-Anon program which served the family members of alcoholics, offering them respite, encouragement and support. Everyone who met Sister Ignatia found her to be non-judgmental in her actions and words. Her mission was to serve those who had need of her.

Thirty years later, Sister Ignatia was still carrying on her work. Her health was beginning to fail so her Congregation decided that she should retire to the Sisters' Motherhouse in May 1965. In April of the following year, Sister Ignatia passed away at the age of seventy-seven years. 3,000 people attended her funeral. She had never been one to accept public praise on her own behalf. The funeral attendees wanted everyone to know that they knew what a special person Sister Ignatia had been in their lives. Even when she had received a proclamation from President John F. Kennedy, she only accepted on behalf of her Congregation and the medical profession. She asked whenever there was another accolade awarded to her that there be "no fuss". She was inducted into the Ohio Women's Hall of Fame as well as the Health Care Hall of Fame. Throughout her years of working with those in the grip of alcohol addiction, and even to this day, she was, and is, known as 'the Angel of Alcoholics Anonymous'.

OKLAHOMA:

Tears Ever Near

Alzira McCaughey Powell Murray

Alzira McCaughey was the daughter of Charles and Sophia Dibrell McCaughey. She was born on February 8, 1849 in Starkville, Oktibbeha County, Mississippi. Her father, born in 1800, was an Irish immigrant from Londonderry, Ireland. Alzira's mother Sophia was born in Tennessee in 1822. Her parents were Charles and Alzira Folsom Dibrell. Alzira had an older brother Emmet and two younger sisters, Hibernian and Talulah plus one younger brother, John. Alzira's maternal great grandmother was Molly Ar-chi-ho-yo Folsom, a member of the indigenous Choctaw tribe. At the time of the Choctaw removal from their ancestral homeland, a time recorded as the Trail of Tears, 1831-1838, Sophia had been moved with her family and thousands of other Choctaw tribal members to land in the western United States known as Indian Territory. The Territory became part of the state of Oklahoma when statehood was conferred in 1907. The members of the Choctaw tribe who refused to leave their homeland came to be known as the Mississippi Band of Choctaw Indians. The grueling walk from Mississippi to Indian Territory claimed 3,000 lives. 70,000 people were forcibly removed from land confiscated from them by an act of the United States Congress and President Andrew Jackson.

In 1863, when Alzira was fourteen years old, her father died from a fever during the siege of Vicksburg, Mississippi. Two years later, Sophia took her children back to Indian Territory where other family members were living. At the age of nineteen, Alzira married William Powell, a captain in the U.S. Army. She gave birth to their daughter Anita one year later. Shortly after her daughter's birth, William died. He was twenty-one years old. Alzira married again the next year. Her husband was Frank Murray. Frank was also an immigrant from Londonderry, Ireland. He had first landed in New Orleans, Louisiana, then worked his way across the land to Indian Territory.

Alzira and Frank took up farming, just as Alzira's mother and siblings did. Many in the Choctaw tribe were excellent farmers as well as skilled traders. They followed the same patterns of planting, irrigating and reaping as their ancestors did. Frank was entitled to take up land in Indian Territory by virtue of his marriage to Alzira. Frank, Alzira and their daughter Anita, moved to Pauls Valley, Indian Territory. They remained here for a time. The family then moved to Erin Springs in the Territory. Their nearest neighbors were twenty-five miles away from their cabin. Frank and Alzira continually built up the amount of land they had until they controlled a ranch in excess of 20,000 acres. At one time, they owned more than 26,000 cattle.

"Lindsay-Murray Mansion" Jim Argo Collection, Courtesy of the Oklahoma Historical Society

After a few years in Erin Springs, Frank and Alzira decided to build a large house, completely from stone, in the middle of their ranch. There was a quarry nearby from where they could obtain the stones. A man named John Coyle, a recent immigrant from Scotland, was hired as the head mason for the construction. The walls of the finished house were eighteen inches thick. The house included a basement and an attic. In total, there were 15 rooms plus multiple bathrooms. The house was the largest and most elaborate building in the Territory. The Murrays were often visited by Territorial Governors, tribal chiefs and military officers passing through the area.

Alzira gave birth to eight children between 1872-1888. Her daughter Erin, born in 1882, was the first of these children to live into her adulthood years. Three more daughters were born after Erin. They were Lula, Ila and Mamie. The children filled Alzira with great joy. She never forgot her children who passed away while still infants or at very young ages. Her daughter Anita married Lewis Lindsay in 1890. Alzira was also involved in the business of running the farm and the ranch. It was a good thing that Alzira did keep on top of business matters because Frank died in 1892. His passing happened during a time of economic downturn in the country. The ranch was not as profitable as it had been. Frank had been deeply in debt. All of the business decisions fell to Alzira now. She cut expenses and managed the farm interests particularly. Slowly, she was able to put the family finances back on track. Alzira realized that running the farm was not the best way for her to keep her finances stable. Instead, she turned to commercial interests. She became a major stockholder of the First National Bank of Lindsay in the Territory as well as a stockholder in other banks. She invested in a mill and grain elevator in nearby Pauls Valley. She owned an interest in the Purcell Electric Light Company.

Education for her children was always a priority for Alzira. She and Frank sent their children to the Catholic schools in Denison, Texas as well as the Sacred Heart Academy. Both schools were many miles from Erin Springs. While on a trip with her firstborn son John to visit two of her daughters away at school in 1897, John passed away. Alzira brought her daughters home. She did not want any more of her children to be far away from her. She enrolled the two girls in a school in Erin Springs. Four years later, both daughters succumbed to scarlet fever. The girls died within one week of each other. Alzira and her daughters Erin and Lula returned to the stone house on the ranch. Only three of Alzira's nine children were still living.

Alzira decided that she would renovate and remodel her large house. She had hope that many grandchildren would fill the rooms. She had the veranda removed so that she could have thick columns installed at the front entrance. The roof was raised, allowing more space in the attic which would be converted to rooms. Alzira's daughter Lula married in 1904 and Erin married in 1905. Two granddaughters were born in the next few years. Alzira's joy in these granddaughters did not assuage the heartache she felt when Lula died in 1914 at the age of thirty years.

In 1919, when Alzira was seventy years old, she suffered a stroke while she was away from home visiting friends in Colorado Springs, Colorado. The stroke left her with limited mobility and paralysis. After six years, on August 3, 1924, Alzira passed away. She was seventy-five years old. She was buried in the cemetery at Erin Springs, now part of the state of Oklahoma, next to all of her children who predeceased her. In Alzira's lifetime, she experienced tragedies over and over again. The forced removal of her mother's family to land and settlement not of their choosing left scars that never healed. Alzira and Frank found a way to turn this tragedy into a triumph, by utilizing the land and its resources. There was no triumph without cost, however. Hard work was a part of every day. Tears were never far away as the deaths of her children often seemed too much to bear. Still, Alzira did not allow herself to stop. She carried on just as her Choctaw family continued to do.

OREGON:

Needle and Thread

Anne Fitzpatrick Armstrong

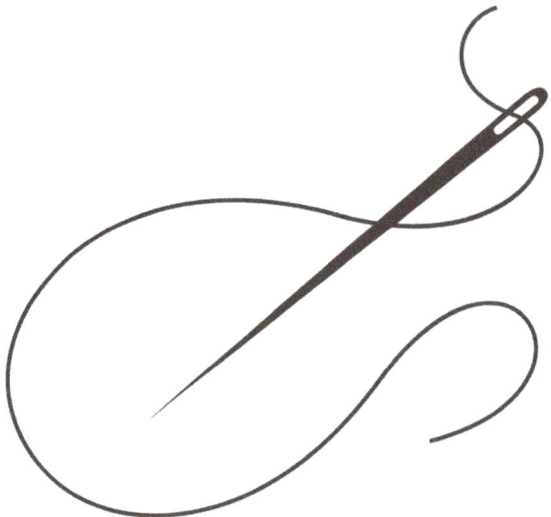

"Needle and Thread" Creator: yegor22 Istock photos.

Anne Fitzpatrick was the youngest of the eight children born to John/Thomas and Ann Leonard Fitzpatrick. She was born on September 13, 1850 in County Cavan, Ireland. When Anne was eighteen years old, she said goodbye to her family and sailed to the United States. This was only a few years after the potato famine of 1845-1852. Most of the Irish people who survived the famine were still desperately poor. Anne had no prospects for earning a living in Ireland. She came ashore in New York City but she did not remain in the city for long. Some of her relatives who had emigrated from Ireland earlier were living in San Francisco, California so Anne made her way across the country where she was reunited with them. These relatives took Anne in, giving her a place to stay. Now, Anne had to find a way to make her living. She turned her hands to dressmaking. Dressmaking could be done in a home rather than a shop. Anne's work caught the eyes of some of the affluent women in the city. They began to order their dresses from her. During the years that Anne lived in San Francisco, she saved the money she earned from making dresses. After seven years, she was ready to strike out on her own in a new place.

Anne moved to the town of Portland in the Oregon Territory. Portland was the largest town in the Territory which encompassed land that included the future state of Washington and parts of Idaho and Montana. People expected Portland to come into its own as an important city, situated as it was between the Columbia and Willamette Rivers. Shipping and freighting were already important industries. There was not a large number of Irish immigrants living in the Territory compared to the East Coast or San Francisco, but more Irish pioneers were arriving every day. Most of the men found work as laborers on the docks or in the lumber industry. Anne believed that her dressmaking skills would be needed as the population grew. She could be her own boss, working in her own home. Otherwise, as a single young woman, her only other option for employment would be in domestic service which would not pay enough money for her to live independently. Industrialization with jobs in manufacturing that were open to women had not yet come to Portland. Women in religious orders had arrived in Portland in order to open schools and to serve in nursing capacities, but Anne did not feel called to a life with the Sisters.

Shortly after arriving in Portland, Anne married a man named James Armstrong. James, born in 1848, was another Irish immigrant. He worked as a laborer in Portland but did not earn enough to support the family. Anne's plan for opening a dressmaking business did not materialize. Instead, James and Anne migrated to British Columbia because James thought his prospects would be better there. Anne gave birth to three children while they were living in British Columbia, though only two children survived. Making ends meet still proved to be very difficult. James and Anne decided to return to Portland with their young children. James found work as a laborer once again. Anne took care of her two surviving children and the house. In 1880, both of the children, Joseph and Mary, were infected with measles. Anne nursed them through their illnesses until they were well again. After this, she decided to take matters into her own hands regarding the family's finances. Most laborers never earned enough money to support a family beyond a meager existence. Anne was confident that her dressmaking skills would be very welcome in Portland even though it was considered unusual for a married woman to take on paid work. She took out her own listing in the Portland City Directory. "Armstrong, Mrs. Anna M, dressmaker 53 N 4th, res same."

Anne was not alone in her choice of profession in Portland by any means. In 1860, there were only two women listed as seamstresses in the town. Ten years later, there were 36 women seamstresses. When Anne took up her needle and thread in 1880, she was one of 246 women carrying on this trade. The population of the city had grown to 17,577. Seamstresses were in high demand. There were plenty of customers coming to Anne's door. These customers were eager to have their dresses be of the latest fashions that were current in New York and San Francisco.

James Armstrong passed away in1895. He and Anne had been married for twenty years. Without James's income, it would be difficult for Anne to provide for Joseph and Mary solely from her income. She decided that it was time for the family to migrate again. This time, they moved to Butte, Montana. The population in Butte was growing every day due to the opening of many copper mines. Anne opened up her dressmaking shop in their new house in Butte. Already, there were many people who could afford to utilize the services of a dressmaker. She was soon very busy. Joseph found work as a carpenter. Mary took a job as a stenographer. Both children graduated from secondary school which made Anne proud. She had always wanted her children to receive a good education.

Anne remained in Butte for the rest of her life. Her daughter Mary married a man named Arthur Vincent Corry, the son of a prominent Butte family in 1903. Mary and Arthur invited Anne to live with them. Their son, Andrew Vincent, was born in 1904. Anne continued with her dressmaking but gradually eased her workload and did not take on new customers. She joined St. Patrick's Catholic Church in Butte where she took on leadership roles for many of the charitable works the church sponsored. At the age of eighty-six, Anne passed away at St. James Hospital in Butte. She was buried in St. Patrick's Cemetery in Butte.

In her younger years, Anne had struck out on her own, traveling to a new country to find a place where she could earn a living on her terms. She made her own way and paid her own way by always carrying with her the tools of her trade. A needle and thread may be small and lightweight, but they were strong enough to help Anne sew together a new life in America.

PENNSYLVANIA:

Letters to My Brother

Hannah Curtis Lynch

Hannah Curtis was born around 1824-1830. Births were not always recorded immediately after a child's birth. She lived in County Laois, Ireland. County Laois was also known as Queens County. She was the daughter of William and Bridget Dunne Curtis. Among her siblings were her brothers John, William and Thomas. She also had two sisters, Margaret and Jane. Like most families in Ireland, the Curtis family was very poor. As each of the children grew, talk of immigration to America was debated and ultimately decided upon as the only way to ever have hope for a better life.

Hannah's brother John immigrated to Philadelphia, Pennsylvania in 1837. He went to live with his uncle, Timothy Dunne, who had immigrated a few years earlier. Timothy took up farming. John wanted to stay in the city. He found work and lodging. It was John's plan to save as much of his earnings as he could so that he could send money home to his parents and siblings in Laois. They would then have the money needed for passage to America. John joined the St. Patrick Beneficent Society which assisted Irish immigrants who came to America. The Society also sent financial aid to people in Ireland.

In July 1845, Hannah's sister Jane wrote a letter to her mother after she arrived in America. John had sent money for Jane to immigrate to Philadelphia. Jane wrote that John had a good job and was earning a good wage. Jane also reported that she had unexpectedly met two of her mother's sisters in the city, Mary Dillon and Margaret Dunne. Jane was so happy to have reunited with relatives! Jane also wrote that John was advising their brother William to delay his immigration because the summer temperatures in the city were so hot. Letters from Jane and John to their parents and siblings kept the dream of immigration for the others alive.

Hannah wrote to John later that same year. She had received a letter from him on the 14th of November. Letters could only be sent on ships going back and forth between the United States and Ireland so many weeks passed before letters arrived at their destinations. Hannah was married by

"Hannah Curtis Lynch Letter to her brother John Curtis" Courtesy Pennsylvania Historical Society

this time. She wrote to let John know that she and her husband, William Lynch, a tailor by trade, had moved into a new house which they were renting for twelve pounds per year. They would keep possession of their former house as well so that William's parents could live there. They also planned to open that house to lodgers which would hopefully bring in more income. Hannah also informed John about the blight that had affected the potato harvest. She wrote, "Dear Brother, it is most dreadful the state the potatoes are in in Ireland and all over the world they are all tainted in the ground it is the opinion of every one there will be no potatoes with everything in very short we are greatly afraid there will be a famine this year if the Lord does not do something for the people they are not aware of every things rates very high at present". She went on to write that while her husband had been making a good living, the situation was deteriorating. "William can employ 10 men and has work for 3 or 4 more only for the way the potatoes has turned out We were very well off we have 2 acres of them sowed this year but they are not good".

The letters that the family members sent to each other also contained news that was in letters from more distant relatives. Hannah and John were both corresponding with their uncle, William Dunne, who lived in Belfast, Ireland with his wife and family. William worked as a groom, caring for the horses gentlemen visitors rode into the city. William mentioned in one of his letters to John, written on April 25, 1846, that there was no longer any work for him or for anyone he knew. William then asked, "Could you gether something let it be Ever so little it would be very Receptable at a time like this people that has friends in America about where I am they are sending them help Everyday but let that not hinder you from riting as we will be glad to here from you and all friends". Both William and Hannah were growing increasingly worried about the state of Ireland and the growing number of people without food or income.

John continued to work hard and to save money. He was able to send the fare for his parents to immigrate in 1846. Bridget and William arrived safely in Philadelphia. His Uncle William wrote to tell him, "There is nothing here but hardship and starvation our potato crop is all used all over Ireland this year but I suppose you have herd of it there was not one stem of potatoes in my house this three months".

Hannah was growing more desperate with each passing day, wondering how she and William would survive. Uncle William had written to Hannah that she should receive a letter from John in March 1847. The promised letter did not arrive until April. Hannah found the waiting very hard. She had written to John, asking that he please send the money for herself and William to book passage to America. "I think you would have no right to forget me when it is in your power. I related to you the state of the Country in that letter therefore I need not go over it any more only the distress that was amongst the people at that time was nothing to what it is at present the people are in a starving state the poor house is crowded with people and they are dying as fast as they can from 10 to 20 a day out of it there is some kind of strange fever in it and it is the opinion of the Doctor it will spread over town and country when the weather grows warm no person can be sure of their lives one moment the times are so sudden you would scarcely see...there is no prospect of any thing here but poverty and distress.."

Hannah had expected that her brother would have sent her the money for passage. Some of her aunts had received money so Hannah and William planned to travel with them. "We sold all our furniture in order to have no delay...what we got for them is not worth mentioning as everything is sold now for half nothing All I kept was the bed and bedclothes that we would want to take with us so now we have nothing but the bare walls of the house".

Hannah wrote that letter on April 21, 1847. By the latter part of April, most Irish families already had their potato sets planted. But that year, there were not any seed potatoes that could be planted. When the potato

135

crop failed in 1845, people had managed by eating the seed potatoes they would have planted in 1846. Unbeknownst to them, those seed potatoes were also infected with the same fungus and so failed again. There were not any seed potatoes to plant in 1847. Hannah wrote, "I thought nothing would make you all forget me and I the only person left alone and from the promises my father made one at the boat that you all would join and send for me in a short time...you need not be saying you would do better at home as you may now what home is I am sure we would do as well as others and if you would only lend us what you could with the help of God we would be able to pay you again perhaps...I trust with the blessing of the Lord we will all meet and spend happy days together...".

Fortunately, Hannah and William were able to immigrate in 1848. John and the other family members were able to combine their money to pay for their passage. Hannah and William were two of the more than 1,000,000 people who emigrated from Ireland during the famine years of 1845-1851. Hannah and William were given an opportunity for a better life which they believed would begin the moment they stepped ashore in Philadelphia. William was able to take on tailoring jobs once again. Hannah found work as a vest maker in a factory. They did not realize riches in America. But they did escape starvation and poverty. The riches they did find were among the family they reunited with in Philadelphia, Pennsylvania.

RHODE ISLAND:

My Turn to Speak

Isabelle Ahearn O'Neill

"Isabelle Ahearn O'Neill" Courtesy of Rhode Island Historical Society

Isabelle Florence Ahearn was the daughter of Daniel Ahearn and Mary J. O'Connor who were both born between 1839-1840. Daniel was born in Rhode Island, the son of Irish immigrants. Mary O'Connor emigrated from County Kerry, Ireland in 1847 with her family. Isabelle's exact birth year was not recorded, although it was between 1880-1883. She was born in Woonsocket, Rhode Island on June 8. Isabelle was the thirteenth and youngest child born into the family. Nine siblings were living at home when Isabelle was born. Daniel Ahearn was a horse trader. This did not pay him much money so the family moved to the town of Providence, Rhode Island. There was enough money for Isabelle to attend the Boston College of Drama and Oratory after finishing secondary school in Providence. While at the college, Isabelle took part in physical education classes as well as elocution classes.

When she returned to Providence after her graduation, she began teaching elocution and physical education classes in a school she founded. She named this school The Ahearn School of Oratory, Drama and Physical Education.

Isabelle and her students presented annual recitals at the Providence Opera House. She lived at home with her parents and her siblings who ranged in age from twenty to forty years. Her brothers worked as salesmen and her sisters all had jobs as dry goods clerks. Her father worked as an auctioneer. Isabelle married when she was about twenty-five years old. Her husband was John A. O'Neill. Their only child was a son John, born in 1908. Young John was only three years old when he passed away from meningitis. Isabelle and her husband had recently separated before young John died. They did not divorce as they were both practicing Catholics and divorce was not allowed according to Catholic doctrine.

Between the years 1900-1918, Isabelle acted in several theater productions in Rhode Island and in New York. She was a member of the New York Dramatic League. She was also a member of the Empire Stock Company. In 1915, she joined the Eastern Film Corporation, a production company that made silent screen films.

Isabelle became a champion and a campaigner for women's suffrage. She joined the Rhode Island Equal Suffrage Association. When the Rhode Island Legislature ratified the Nineteenth Amendment of the U.S. Constitution, legalizing voting rights for women, Isabelle joined the United League of Women Voters. The United League of Women Voters supported women who wished to learn more about governance and politics. Isabelle enrolled in the League's School of Government Procedure. She entered into political discussions and campaigned for Democratic candidates. In 1922, Isabelle was the first woman in Rhode Island to chair a Democratic Party rally in support of gubernatorial candidate William S. Flynn. Flynn won the governor's seat in 1922.

Governor Flynn was not the only candidate to win in that year. Isabelle won a seat in the Rhode Island Legislative General Assembly. She had given over 100 campaign speeches. The *Providence Journal* announced her win stating, "hers were some of the best speeches of the campaign. And she did it without a physical setback." Isabelle had shown that a woman campaigning against men for an important legislative position was not too weak, nor too intimidated, for the task. In her new position, Isabelle kept the concerns of women and children in front of the other legislators. She gave speeches condemning child labor. She supported equal pay for women teachers as well as teacher pensions. She let it be known that women were competent and capable of jury duty as well as holding positions in public office.

Isabelle did not always agree with stances the Democratic Party took on some issues. She disagreed that Prohibition should be repealed. She voted to create a Rhode Island State Police force, a stand not favored by many other party members. Even so, her colleagues held her in high regard. She was a delegate to the Democratic National Convention in 1924, 1928 and 1932. She also served on many political committees.

After four terms as a legislator in the House of Representatives, Isabelle successfully won a seat in the Rhode Island Senate in 1930. She was elected as deputy floor leader, another first for a woman in state government. She was re-elected in 1932. In 1933, Isabelle resigned from her senate seat in order to accept an appointment by President Franklin Roosevelt to the newly formed U.S. Bureau of Narcotics. Isabelle remained in this position for ten years.

In 1943, Isabelle returned to Providence to live with her older sister Mary Ann. Mary Ann was in need of care due to the onset of blindness. Isabelle took a job with the Rhode Island Department of Labor. She worked as a cost of living investigator with the department for ten years. She retired at the age of seventy-three. Isabelle lived in Providence for twenty more years until her death on March 17, 1975. She was ninety-four years old. In 2011, the Rhode Island YWCA created the Isabelle Ahearn O'Neill Award which honors women leaders of Rhode Island. Isabelle was inducted into the Rhode Island Heritage Hall of Fame in 2014. Isabelle used her voice throughout all of her life. As a young woman, her voice entertained audiences. As a legislator and civil servant, her voice promoted causes that Isabelle knew were important, not just for women but for everyone.

SOUTH CAROLINA:
An Unmarked Grave

Ellen O'Driscoll O'Donovan

Unmarked graves and forgotten stories were the fate of many Irish immigrants who emigrated from Ireland with a hope for a new and better life. The men who did find fame and wealth and glory were portrayed in biographical portrait albums of the time. Rarely was a woman mentioned in those albums. Sometimes, the wife of a prominent man had a few lines written about her, usually stating that she was supportive and helpful to her husband. The parents and grandparents of these important men might also be mentioned as they were thought to be the people who had molded and formed the man. One celebrated Irishman whose life touched everyone in Ireland in the latter part of the 19th century and early years of the 20th century, did give praise to his mother. She, however, upon her passing, was one of the many buried in an unmarked grave.

Ellen O'Driscoll was the daughter of Cornelius and Anna O'Leary O'Driscoll. She was born around the year 1798 in Reenascreena, Rosscarbery, County Cork, Ireland. Ellen, or Nellie, as she was known, was the eldest of eleven children. Nellie grew up in a home where the Irish language was the first language of everyone living there, as well as most of their neighbors. Use of the English language occurred only when the English landlord or his agent came through collecting the rent for the land the family lived on and farmed.

When Nellie was fifteen years old, she and Denis O'Donovan of Cooragreenane, County Cork married. According to her son Jeremiah's recollections in his autobiography, Nellie was standing along the roadside with some other girls one evening when Denis came along upon his horse. Denis was returning home from the market fair held at Ross. The girls hailed Denis and "challenged him for a faireen." Denis tossed a guinea coin towards the girls. Nellie caught the coin in her hand. The gold piece was the talk of the girls afterwards. A few days later, Denis proposed marriage to Nellie. Nellie's parents visited Denis's parents at their house. Cooragreenane was only one mile north of Nellie's house in Reenascreena. The two families approved of each other and the match was made. Nellie and Denis married soon after in 1818.

Nellie gave birth to four children, John, Jeremiah, Cornelius and Mary. Jeremiah was sent to live with Ellen's parents and siblings on their farm when he was almost four years old. He remained with his grandparents until he reached the age of seven. Nellie wanted one of her children to experience their young years as she had done. During this time, Denis worked as a tenant farmer on land owned by Thomas Hungerford of Cahirmore. There was never much money, but there was enough food, thanks to the potatoes grown on their small plot of land. Denis paid the yearly rent in other crops that he grew on this land. The children were able to attend school.

In 1845, people in the locality were saying that the potatoes growing in the fields were rotting. Nellie, Denis and Jeremiah went to check their own field. They saw that the potato stalks had withered, but under the ground, the potatoes seemed to be of a good size. They dug all of the potatoes out and then buried them in a pit near the field. Their neighbors were all doing the same thing. When they went to check on their potatoes later, they found that most of them were rotting. They quickly separated the few remaining good potatoes, carrying them to a storage shed behind the house. They padded the shed with straw to keep out any moisture. Before long, Nellie noticed that these potatoes were also rotting. This time, when they separated the remaining good potatoes from the bad, they carried them inside the house to a loft above the kitchen. These potatoes also rotted. The entire potato crop, meant to feed the family for a year, was gone.

The other crop in the family's rented field was wheat. The landlord assigned keepers to guard the wheat at harvest time. This wheat was meant to pay the rent Nellie and her family owed to the landlord. The keepers stayed in the family home to make sure none of the wheat was taken for the family's use. One of the keepers accompanied Nellie to the nearby mill when she took the wheat to be ground. From the mill, Nellie and the keeper walked to the landlord's agent's stall in the town. The agent was there to collect the yearly rent for the landlord. The O'Donovan's rent was 18 pounds per year. From the twelve bags of wheat harvested, Nellie had been paid 18 pounds and 5 shillings. The agent took all of the money. Nellie walked home without any money for her family.

Since Denis was a tenant farmer, he could apply for relief during this time through the Poor Law which would give a farmer money for his family, but only if he forfeited his tenancy claim. The land would be returned to the landlord. Instead of this, Denis found employment under the Board Of Works Law. An applicant would be put to work building public works. Denis was in charge of a work crew building a new road in the locality. The work was grueling. The men received very little food. Denis grew weaker each day. Eventually, he became too ill and weak to manage his crew. His son Jeremiah was told to take Denis's place until Denis recovered. One day, the overseer of the road crews came to find Jeremiah. He told Jeremiah that he was wanted at home. Jeremiah hurried home to find that Denis had died from 'famine fever'. Without Denis to support the family, Nellie and the children were evicted from their holding in May 1847. The creditors came and removed everything from inside the house, depositing it at the roadside. The family moved into a neighbor's house which had once been both a house and a shop. The house was available because the neighbor had died, a victim of the famine. There was a big window at the front of the house where the former shop owner had displayed his wares. After Nellie moved into the house, she awoke one morning to find some of the patrolling English police force had pasted writings on the window. The signs disparaged a group of young Irishmen who had traveled to Paris to offer congratulations upon the beginning of a new Republic in France. Nellie took down the signs and tore them into shreds. She was not going to have her domicile appear to support English views of the Irish. For a few months, one of Nellie's relatives brought the family a load of turf to burn for heat and a bag of flour with which to make bread. One day, Nellie's relative no longer came. He too became one of the famine's victims. Now there was nothing to eat and no way to keep warm.

Fortunately for Nellie and her family, one of Denis's brothers, Cornelius, along with his wife and children, had immigrated to Philadelphia, Pennsylvania a few years earlier in 1841. Since they had settled there, Cornelius had begun sending money to the family in Ireland so that more of the O'Donovans could immigrate to Philadelphia. Nellie's son John left first. She then sent her son Cornelius to live with her parents. Jeremiah was sent to live with an aunt and uncle in Skibbereen, County Cork. Jeremiah was put to work in a hardware shop. By the year 1848, John O'Donovan had saved enough money to send for Nellie, Cornelius and Mary to immigrate. As hard as it was for Nellie to leave her homeland, she was determined to save her children from a famine fate.

Jeremiah traveled back from Skibbereen to Reenascreena to bid his family farewell. He walked with them to the place where the other immigrating families were gathering. All of them were heading to the harbor in the city of Cork. With tears and cries, the families parted. Jeremiah walked backwards toward Skibbereen, trying to watch his family until they were completely out of his sight. He wrote later, "I don't forget my mother, a tall, straight, handsome woman, when I was a child: looking stately in the long, hooded cloak she used to wear…" He did not know if he would ever see any of his family again.

Nellie and the two children survived the ocean crossing. When they reached Philadelphia, they lived with her son John and his family for several years. When her daughter married a man named Walter Webb, Nellie moved into their home. Walter was a police officer. He had first been on the force in New York City before coming to Philadelphia.

"West Cork Shawl" Courtesy Rosscarbery Historical Society

Back in Ireland, Jeremiah, who called himself O'Donovan Rossa now, was becoming quite well known among the Fenians. The Fenians were Irish men who wanted to free Ireland from England's rule. They vowed to use force if necessary. Jeremiah delivered stirring speeches which led other men to join the Fenians. Eventually, Jeremiah was able to visit America in 1863. He went to Philadelphia to visit Nellie and his siblings. It was dark outside when Jeremiah arrived at his brother John's house. He knocked on the door. Nellie answered the knocking. She did not recognize Jeremiah. Jeremiah told Nellie that it was himself who was there. She still did not believe him until she reached up and touched the scar on his head-a result of a fall when he had been a young boy. Jeremiah noticed that Nellie had changed greatly in appearance as well. The next morning, in the daylight, Jeremiah said, "I saw her the next morning, with a yankee shawl and bonnet, looking as old as my grandmother..." Nellie visited with Jeremiah during the week he spent in Philadelphia. She never saw him again after that visit.

Nellie moved with Mary and Walter to Charleston, South Carolina. Walter continued working as a police officer. Nellie was nearly seventy years old. She had survived tragedies and years of hard work. She was not expecting any recognition in Charleston because she did not know anyone there. When it was learned that she was a new resident of the city, Nellie became instantly well known. The fame of her son Jeremiah had preceded her. Jeremiah was famous throughout Ireland and the United States for his speeches proclaiming Ireland should be free from England's rule. Many of his speeches were printed and were widely read. He had been imprisoned for many years due to the nature of his publications, speeches and activities in the cause for Ireland's freedom. To like-minded Irish nationalists, Jeremiah was a hero.

The Fenian leadership in Charleston wanted to honor Nellie because she was the mother of one of Ireland's greatest sons. They organized a meeting which was held on April 18, 1870. It was reported, "The chairman explained that the meeting was called for the purpose of adopting measures for the relief of the mother of O'Donovan Rossa who is now in the city in a destitute condition." The chairman went on to say that since Jeremiah O'Donovan Rossa was in prison for life for his actions on behalf of the Irish people, it was the duty of those present to care for his mother since Jeremiah could not do so himself.

The warm welcome the Charleston Irish community gave to Nellie was a great comfort to her. The high temperatures of the summer months in Charleston were difficult for her. Her body weakened. On September 1, 1870, Nellie passed away from typhoid fever. The *Charleston Daily News* announced her passing.

"Death of Mrs. Donovan Rossa. This aged and respected lady who is the mother of the distinguished Irish martyr now wearing out an inglorious sentence in a British prison when his valor and eloquence might be illustrated in the cause of his country, took place yesterday, at five o'clock, at the residence of her son-in-law, Walter Webb, Esq, No 32 King Street, where she received every kindness a limited means would permit."

Nellie was buried in St. Lawrence Cemetery in Charleston. There was not any money for a headstone to mark her grave. The local Irish community formed a committee to gather donations for a suitable monument to be erected over the grave of the mother of one of Ireland's foremost patriots. The appeal for donations was made but no monument was ever erected. Nellie's life closed without fanfare but not without note as one who helped to shape the son who championed Ireland's cause for freedom.

SOUTH DAKOTA:

Starting Over Again and Again

Catherine Fitzgerald Dinneen

Many Irish immigrants did not settle in one place once they reached North America. While East Coast cities like New York City or Boston or Philadelphia or Baltimore were the usual ports where immigrants landed, these cities were very crowded. It was difficult to find lodgings and work. In Canada, the usual ports for disembarking were Quebec or Peterborough or in Simcoe County. These places too became dense with people. Immigrants who wished to buy farmland had to travel west. Those who wanted to try their luck in mining minerals had to travel west as well. Some immigrants wanted to be among the first to settle in an area. They wanted to be part of a growing town or community. Part of the allure of North America was the freedom of movement Irish immigrants found. They had enjoyed no such freedom back in Ireland.

Catherine Fitzgerald was the daughter of Michael and Catherine Quinn Fitzgerald. She was born in 1843. Her parents had immigrated to Quebec from Ireland in the mid 1830s with their two sons, Edmund and Patrick. When Catherine was one year old, the family migrated to Franklin County, New York. Migrating from Canada to the United States was as simple as walking across the land border. Many people moved back and forth freely between the two countries as their fortunes took them. Three younger brothers were born while Catherine was growing up in Franklin County. When she was sixteen years old, Catherine and Michael Dinneen married. Michael was an Irish immigrant from Fermoy, County Cork. He had come to the United States with his parents, Dennis and Catherine Callaghan Dinneen, when he was two years old in 1835. Michael's father was a farmer. Michael and his siblings grew up on the family farm where they were all expected to put in a day's work every day.

Catherine gave birth to three sons while she and Michael lived in New York. In 1866, the family migrated west to New Ulm, Stark County, Minnesota. Michael purchased 400 acres of land. He planned to grow wheat. It took many years for Michael, Catherine and now five sons to improve their land enough to realize a prosperous farm. The family was pleased with their success but felt the lack of a Catholic Church anywhere in their vicinity. Two years after their arrival, Catherine and Michael joined with the other Catholic followers in New Ulm to build a church. After this church was built, the group built a church at Sleepy Eye, Minnesota, then another church in the town of Leavenworth.

Michael was not satisfied that he had taken his family as far as they could go in prosperity. He began looking around with the idea of moving once again. Michael and his oldest son, Maurice, rode the train to the town of Volga, in the Dakota Territory in March 1880. Volga was the end of the line for the train service. From Volga, the two men rode horseback to the settlement at Huron, Dakota Territory. They filed two tree claims which gave them land they would own after they had planted trees on at least ten acres of each claim. Carrying a copy of the officially recorded claims, father and son returned home to plant their crops for the season. By May 1881, the entire family had arrived in Huron. They settled in the town. Michael purchased the building known as the Dakota Hotel. He renamed the building, 'The James River Hotel' due to Huron's location on the James River. Catherine and Michael set to work renovating the building.

"Blizzard" Created 1936 by Rothstein, Arthur, photographer https://www.loc.gov/resource/FSU.8b27548/ Public Domain through Unsplash

When some of the family migrated to Huron in the autumn of 1880, they brought with them most of their cattle and hogs. This proved to be providential when a blizzard struck the town and surrounding area in October. There was deep snow all around. Many more severe winter storms struck throughout the winter months. The Chicago and Northwestern Railroad suspended train service until springtime. No supply trains could get to the people stranded by the blizzard. The forced confinement lasted until the end of April 1881. In many places, the snow reached the height of the housetops. Catherine cooked many meals for their neighbors from their cattle and hogs. She helped to keep the townspeople from starving. Catherine shared the butter she churned from the cows' milk. She prepared meals to be delivered to those who had very little to eat and no means to pay for food. On one of Catherine's delivery runs, she nearly lost her life when the horse pulling her wagon reared, causing the buggy to overturn. Catherine salvaged the food and delivered the meals to a family with seven hungry children.

Working on the hotel took both a great deal of time and money. During her second year in Huron, Catherine gave her diamond wedding ring as collateral for a loan which she and Michael needed to continue to provide for their family and to finish the work on the hotel. In the summer of 1883, the hotel renovation was completed. The Dinneens opened their hotel for business.

A short while later, a Catholic priest rode into Huron. His name was Father Robert Haire. Catherine offered to Father Haire the use of the hotel for church services. Father Haire accepted her offer. He held Mass in the hotel every Sunday for three years. Meanwhile, Catherine and Michael began to buy adjoining lots in the town for the eventual building of a Catholic Church. Michael took on a great deal of debt in order to have the necessary supplies for the construction of the church. When the building was completed in 1887, the chief carpenter locked the door and pocketed the key. He would not give up the key until he had been paid in full for the work. He was owed $280.

The money was not available. The Catholics in town met with Father Haire. He wanted some men to go along with him to the bank manager to see if they could get another loan to pay the carpenter. One of the men accompanying Father Haire told the bank manager that he would offer security for the loan. The bank manager refused. He told Father Haire that he should bring Michael Dinneen back with him-that Michael could stand as security for the loan. Michael did not want to do this because of the amount of debt he already owed. The bank manager told Father Dinneen, "Get Mrs Dinneen to sign the notes." Father Haire went to visit Catherine. He found her working on the accounts in the hotel office. Father Haire explained the difficulty in taking out another loan. Cathrine did not think that she should sign any loan note because it might transpire that Michael would be responsible for repayment. Instead, she had an idea for an alternate plan. Catherine suggested to Father Haire that he return to the bank manager and tell him that if the bank would give him $280, he would pay back whatever amount he could on the first day of every month until the debt was settled. Catherine said that she could sign such a lending note as that. Father Haire was doubtful but returned to the bank. The bank manager was surprised when Father Haire presented this idea. He said to Father Haire, "Whose idea was this?" One of the cashiers said, "I bet it was Mrs. Dinneen's." The bank manager then said, "Father Haire, we will let you have the money."

Catherine wanted all of her sons to have a solid formal education. She and Michael sent the boys to St. Mary's College in Kansas. The Dinneens were financial supporters when it was time to build a new church on the college campus. Catherine was considered a well educated woman. She was often asked to perform readings in Huron and the neighboring towns.

Michael passed away on February 7, 1913. Catherine continued to manage the hotel until her death three years later. She was seventy-three years old. She was taken ill while on a trip to California. She passed away shortly after returning home to Huron, on January 14, 1916. She and Michael were buried in St. Martin's Cemetery in Huron. Like so many other immigrant settlers, Catherine lived in a number of places for years at a time. She did not shy away from leaving all of the people she knew in each place, or all that she had been a part of, to start over again. Each time she came to a new place, she worked tirelessly for her family, while at the same time, extending her generosity to all who were in need.

TENNESSEE:

Votes for Women

Catherine Talty Kenny

"Catherine Talty Kenny"
Courtesy of Tennessee State Museum

Catherine Talty was born in 1874 in Chattanooga, Tennessee. Her parents were Hugh and Bridget Cotter Talty. Catherine's father emigrated from County Clare, Ireland. Her mother was an immigrant from County Kildare, Ireland. When Catherine was four years old, her father passed away during an epidemic of yellow fever which swept through the town. Bridget was left to raise six children, all under the age of ten years. The family did not have much money. Like many other families, they lived in a section of Chattanooga known as Irish Hill. Bridget worked as a seamstress to support her family. She and children moved many times among the tenement buildings in the neighborhood. All of the children found employment as soon as they were old enough to be hired. When Catherine was fifteen years old, the local parish priest arranged for her to attend a convent school in Kentucky instead of joining the labor force. Her opportunity for formal education was short-lived. After one term at Nazareth Academy, Catherine was called home. Her mother needed her to leave the school and find work. During the next ten years, Catherine had a number of jobs. She was, at times, a store clerk, a stenographer and a cashier.

In 1899, Catherine and John Michael Kenny married. The society page of the *Chattanooga Times* newspaper covered the wedding event in detail. It was reported that all of Catherine's friends wished the couple well. The reporter also noted, "Very few girls enjoy the popularity which has been the birthright of Miss Talty. Over all who know her she has exerted the charm of a sweet, generous, kindly nature, with impulses which caused spontaneous admiration from all who met her." Catherine and John made their home in Nashville. John worked as a salesman for a wholesale coffee company. He soon moved on when he received a charter granting him permission to open a Nashville franchise of the Coca-Cola Bottling Company.

The franchise prospered, allowing John and Catherine to move into a larger house. Catherine gave birth to four children during the next thirteen years. As well as being a devoted mother to her children, she also took care of her own mother who was in a frail state. Catherine's mother lived with her family until her death in 1908.

The success of the bottling franchise increased the Kenny's economic standing and their social standing in Nashville. Catherine joined some of the civic organizations for women. She joined the Nashville Equal Suffrage League in 1913. She was the only Roman Catholic member of the League. Many devout Catholics were not able to reconcile their belief that women should only concern themselves with raising children and taking care of the family home with the idea of women's suffrage. Catherine felt that she remained faithful to her Catholic upbringing while supporting the suffrage movement. In one speech that she made in the city of Atlanta, Georgia, Catherine said, "I have the best job in the world. I am the mother of four children, and I'm trying to rear them as they should be reared. I wouldn't give up that job for any position that might be tendered me. But I do want to say something about the conditions under which those children shall be educated, the surroundings in which they must work and the manner in which the laws looking to the removal of temptations from their paths are enforced."

Catherine became acquainted with other women involved in the suffrage movement. Most of the other women were members of Protestant religious denominations. At a time when Protestants and Roman Catholics did not usually serve on the same committees, or even meet socially, Catherine became friends with those other like-minded women. The other women in the League helped Catherine learn to be a speaker and a leader. She became the spokesperson for both the local suffrage organization and the state organization. Eventually, Catherine organized what came to be known as the first suffrage march in the southern states of the United States on May 2, 1914.

One year later, Catherine and another supporter, Abby Crawford Milton, worked together on the campaign committee of the Tennessee Equal Suffrage Association. One of their missions was to organize women's suffrage organizations throughout the state of Tennessee. Even though more women and men were now in support of women's suffrage throughout the country, a long political battle continued. President Woodrow Wilson gave his support to a constitutional amendment guaranteeing women the right to vote. The proposed 19th Amendment to the U.S. Constitution was gaining momentum around the country.

On May 21, 1919, the U.S. House of Representatives passed the 19th Amendment. The U.S. Senate passed the amendment two weeks later. Now, it was up to the individual states to ratify the amendment. Three-fourths of the forty-eight states were required to ratify the amendment in order for it to become law. Catherine was elected head of the ratification committee for the Tennessee Equal Suffrage League. Tennessee Governor Albert H. Roberts was so impressed with Catherine, he called for a special session of the Tennessee General Assembly. The elected Assembly would cast the votes yay or nay for ratification. Catherine planned to have the members of the suffrage committee personally lobby every member of the Assembly. Her leadership and organizational skills, as well as her unfaltering belief that the amendment would be ratified, encouraged the others on the committee to remain dedicated to the cause. Their efforts were rewarded. The Tennessee General Assembly voted in favor of ratification on August 18, 1920. Tennessee was the 36th state to ratify the 19th Amendment. 36 states were needed to equal three-fourths of the 48 states in the Union. Tennessee became known as 'the perfect 36'. The 19th Amendment was signed into law.

While the 19th Amendment guaranteed American women the right to vote, in 1920, this did not include all American women. African American women, indigenous women and other marginalized minorities were not allowed to vote. The struggle to include all American women continued for many more years.

After the passage of the 19th Amendment, Catherine served as the second president of the Tennessee League of Women Voters. Governor Roberts rewarded Catherine's efforts by appointing her chairman of the Nashville City Hospital Commission. Under her leadership of eight years, working conditions for nurses and other employees were improved.

John Kenny passed away in 1926. Catherine decided to move to Brooklyn, New York where her oldest son, John, was living. She remained in Brooklyn for the rest of her life. Catherine passed away in 1950 at the age of seventy-six years. In her lifetime, she cast her vote to move forward the cause for equal rights for women.

TEXAS:

Holding Onto the Land

Elizabeth O'Leary Hart

In 1825, the Government of Mexico passed the Colonization Act in order to encourage settlement by foreign immigrants in the northern region of Mexico which included the states of Coahuila and Texas. Government representatives entered into contracts with twenty-five land agents known as empresarios. The men first attested their loyalty lay with the Mexican government. They were then charged with bringing upstanding families into Texas who were Catholic and who would conduct business in the Spanish language. One of the empresarios was James Power of County Wexford, Ireland. He and his partner, James Hewetson, planned to sign up 200 families for immigration to the Refugio Colony which would be located in the Nueces Strip. The Nueces Strip was located in southern Texas between the Rio Grande and Nueces Rivers.

Power and Hewetson's contract encompassed the years 1828-1834. James Power set out for County Wexford in October 1833. He was a charismatic speaker. He regaled interested potential emigres with descriptions of Texas as a 'paradise on Earth'. He promised that all of the immigrants would own their own land. He told the crowd gathered around him, "Texas is one of the richest countries in the world...with gold so plentiful you could pick it up under the trees." Two of the people listening to his words were Rosalie Hart and her father Thomas Hart. Thomas, especially, was eager to sign on for the new colony. He had previously been employed as a water guard at a lighthouse at Roches Point, County Cork, Ireland. He made a fortune turning over smuggled goods to the English government. His wife, Elizabeth Hart, was not pleased with his employment. She had been given fifty acres of land by her father in County Wexford. She convinced Thomas that he should take up farming on the land. Unfortunately, Thomas had very little knowledge about farming. The farm did not prosper. His daughter Rosalie said about her father, "He was very generous, and he knew nothing of the value of money...he was often applied to for assistance." The result of this was that the family wealth of $25,000 was depleted in three years. Thomas signed the family up for the Refugio Colony.

Elizabeth, Thomas and their three daughters, along with 345 other immigrants sailed in January 1834. The journey across the ocean lasted six weeks. When the ship reached New Orleans, Louisiana, the city population was in the midst of a cholera epidemic. The newly arrived immigrants were directed to smaller boats which would carry them across the gulf to Texas. Thomas Hart and 120 others died from cholera shortly after the group reached Texas. The remaining immigrants were quarantined at the harbor for two weeks. Five year old Elizabeth Hart died from heatstroke during the quarantine. Elizabeth, along with her two daughters, still planned to claim her land in the Refugio Colony.

When the immigrants finally reached the mission at Refugio, there were not any accommodations for them. Elizabeth created a makeshift shelter against one of the walls of the Catholic Church by stacking their belongings around them. Elizabeth acted as a nurse for many of the weakened settlers. She was fortunate that she did not become ill herself, especially during an outbreak of dysentery. Many more of the immigrants died. Elizabeth and the other survivors managed to construct rough huts. They dug trenches, then stood wooden poles upright to form an enclosure. There were no windows and only a dirt floor. Elizabeth and the others were able to plant a few crops. Elizabeth earned a little money milking cows.

With the contract deadline approaching, there were now less than 200 Irish immigrants in Refugio. James Power implored people who were just passing through the area to instead settle in the colony. The governor of the state of Texas made an allowance to the contract allowing immigrants from other countries to join the Irish colony. This concession allowed many more people to settle in Refugio. In time, the number of people immigrating to Texas began to outnumber the population of native Texans. The Mexican government decided to halt any more immigration into the region. Property taxes were raised. Tariffs on goods shipped from the United States were increased. Many settlers and business people were angered. They began to call for Texas to declare its independence from Mexico. General Santa Anna, the President of Mexico, led an army to Texas to put down any attempt at independence. Stephen Austin, who owned thousands of acres in Texas, which he had populated with settlers from the United States, raised an army to engage Santa Anna.

The Irish men, along with others in the Refugio settlement, went to defend a nearby fort when word of war with Santa Anna came to them. Instead of remaining loyal to Mexico, the settlers were in favor of Texan independence. They mostly wanted to keep their land. Santa Anna's army had already won a battle at another fort, the Alamo. Now, the large army headed for Fort Labardee where the Refugio men waited. All of the Refugio men were captured and killed. The women and children remaining at the Refugio Mission had to flee in the night. James Power sent two of his nephews, Tom Conners and John O'Brien, only seventeen and thirteen years, to help the colonists escape. They came with three ox carts. Rosalie Hart wrote in her diary of their escape. "We were ordered to take nothing but provisions for two days and one frying pan, one coffee pot, and a skillet. We were also allowed to take one change of clothing. They would not tell us where we were going...Everybody buried their valuables before leaving...That night teamsters put feather beds on the wagons for the sick, and the others had to walk. It was a sorrowful sight to see so many women and children driven from their homes, and not one in the crowd ever recovered anything that was left behind."

The group walked for days before reaching the settlement of Victoria. They hid in the brush and slept on the ground. The temperature was very cold with constant rain. The group had to keep moving to get away from the fighting. They made it to Dimit's Landing on the banks of the Guadalupe River. There was an eating house there run by a family. Elizabeth offered to help cook if she and her daughters could sleep inside the house. Everyone else slept outside. After a few days' rest, the group had to move again. They made their way to a place where they could cross the Guadalupe River. After walking over swampy ground, they came to Cox's Point. Here, they hoped to find a boat that would take them to the town of Matagorda. In Matagorda, they would try to find a boat that would carry them to New Orleans. The boat, *Tensaw*, was available to take the group. Elizabeth and her daughters thought they were safe. But, the *Tensaw* was followed by a pirate ship soon after it left Matagorda. The captain extinguished all lights and changed course for Mobile, Alabama.

Daily life was safer for Elizabeth and the others in Mobile regarding warring factions, but in another way, danger still lurked closeby. Yellow fever was rampant in Mobile. Many people died. Elizabeth used her nursing skills to care for many people in the town. She was paid $45 per month for nursing. When she was called to attend a person with a more serious case, she was paid an additional $5 per day. Everyone in Mobile who knew Elizabeth respected her highly. She could not save all of the sick people, but she did save many. Among those she could not save was her youngest daughter, Mary Ann.

IRISH IMMIGRANTS IN REFUGIO

THE HISTORY OF SETTLEMENT IN REFUGIO IS CLOSELY ASSOCIATED WITH BALLYGARRETT COUNTY WEXFORD, IRELAND. IRISH NATIVES JAMES POWER (C1788-1852) AND JAMES HEWETSON (1796-1870), BOTH OF WHOM IMMIGRATED TO THE UNITED STATES IN THE EARLY 19TH CENTURY AND LATER BECAME CITIZENS OF MEXICO, OBTAINED PERMISSION FROM THE MEXICAN GOVERNMENT TO OVERSEE THE IMMIGRATION OF MORE THAN 200 IRISH FAMILIES TO TEXAS IN THE 1830s.

THE FIRST GROUP OF IRISH SETTLERS ARRIVED ON THE TEXAS GULF COAST IN 1834. A CHOLERA EPIDEMIC AND THE LOSS OF PROVISIONS AND EQUIPMENT IN ROUGH WATERS AS THE IMMIGRANTS REACHED THE SHORE DELAYED THEIR ARRIVAL IN REFUGIO, WHERE THEY WERE TO SETTLE NEAR THE FORMER SPANISH MISSION OF NUESTRA SENORA DEL REFUGIO. THE COLONY SOON WAS ESTABLISHED, HOWEVER, AND ALMOST IMMEDIATELY THE NEW SETTLERS WERE EMBROILED IN THE CAUSE OF TEXAS INDEPENDENCE FROM MEXICO. MANY IRISHMEN FOUGHT IN THE TEXAS ARMY AND LATER SERVED IN THE REPUBLIC OF TEXAS CONGRESS.

THE IRISH PEOPLE ESTABLISHED A LASTING PRESENCE IN THE REFUGIO AREA. MANY DESCENDANTS OF THE EARLY IMMIGRANTS STILL RESIDE IN THE AREA, SOME ON LAND GRANTED TO THEIR ANCESTORS IN THE 1830s.

"Refugio Colony Memorial Plaque"
Courtesy The Historical Marker Database
Public Domain Image

157

In 1838, Elizabeth decided that her remaining daughter Rosalie would go to a boarding school four miles outside of Mobile. The school was run by Catholic Sisters. Rosalie did not want to leave her mother. Elizabeth assured her that she could come home after the first term if she did not find the school to her liking. Elizabeth wanted Rosalie to receive an education that would serve her well throughout her life. She thought that someday Rosalie might have to earn her own living just as Elizabeth was doing.

When the war ended, Texas was granted its independence from Mexico. The Republic of Texas was officially recognized on March 2, 1836. Fortunately for Elizabeth and the other Refugio colonists, the government of Texas honored the regional land grants of the empresarios. Elizabeth often traveled from Mobile to New Orleans to Refugio in order to make sure that her land grant was still secure. In 1844, Elizabeth decided to permanently settle in the town of Corpus Christi, Texas. The United States annexed the Republic of Texas the following year. The annexation angered the Mexican government as well as many people living in Texas. Others living in the territory wanted Texas to become a state in the Union. The annexation began the Mexican-American War which lasted until 1848. After the war, Texas, as well as 55% of land previously governed by Mexico, came under U.S. jurisdiction.

Elizabeth established a ranch on the Paplote Creek. She eventually owned 4,200 acres of land near Corpus Christi. She established a mercantile store in the town which included a house as well. Rosalie graduated from the convent school near Mobile. She married Jean Marie Priour who had worked at the school as a groundskeeper. Rosalie and her family eventually moved to Corpus Christi where they lived with Elizabeth. Elizabeth bought 500 head of cattle and more land. Her ranch and her business in town both prospered.

People said of Elizabeth that she was a woman of determination and her word was absolute. She was known to help anyone in need. She retired to her ranch as she was approaching her sixth decade. Here, she lived out her remaining days. When she died on December 20, 1863, she was buried underneath the big oak tree near her house. From the moment the ship sailed from Wexford, Elizabeth was committed to holding onto the land she and her family were promised. Nothing swayed her from her conviction, not the deaths of her husband and two daughters, nor the war she found herself in the middle of, running for her life. She concentrated on helping those around her, even when the aid she brought put her own life into danger. Elizabeth did achieve her dream of holding onto her land.

UTAH:

The Woman in Charge of the Money

Jennie Judge Kearns

"Jennie Judge Kearns" Courtesy Park City Museum, Pop Jenks Collection, Park City, Utah

Jennie Judge was born on November 30, 1869 in Port Henry, New York. Her parents were Patrick and Sarah Jane Pattinson Judge. Her father's family emigrated from Ireland in 1846 during the potato famine. Patrick Judge died when Jennie was only two years old. Her mother remarried. Her second husband was William Wilson. When Jennie was ten years old, the family, including Jennie's stepsister, Francis, moved to Park City, Utah where Jennie's uncle, John Judge was living. John Judge was a miner and an engineer. He was the mine superintendent at the Daly Mine in Empire Canyon, Utah.

Jennie had been attending school in Port Henry. She continued her education in Park City. In June 1883, John Judge introduced Jennie to a young man named Thomas Kearns. Tom was born in Canada to Irish immigrants. They were Thomas and Margaret Maher Kearns. The Kearns family migrated from Canada to the Irish settlement in O'Neill, Nebraska where they took up farming. When he had finished with schooling, Tom worked as a freighter, transporting supplies to mining camps. He became interested in mining and so took a job with the Ontario Mine Company in Park City. His boss was a man named David Keith. David gave Tom books to read about mining. When David accepted a contract to dig a tunnel in the nearby Woodside Mine, Tom went along too. While underground, Tom struck a significant vein of silver. He and David formed a partnership to explore the area for more silver lodes. Eventually, they operated a number of mines. They formed the Silver King Coalition Mine in Park City in 1889. The following year, Jennie and Tom married.

Tom, David, Jennie's Uncle John and two other men formed a partnership in order to extend a tunnel shaft in the Mayflower Mine which they were leasing at the time. When the tunnel was 200 feet deep, they struck silver ore. The men quickly bought the Mayflower Mine claim, as well as two other mines. They formed the Silver King Mining Company in July 1892. A few months later, Jennie gave birth to their first child, Margaret, named for Tom's mother. Margaret lived for only nine months before succumbing to scarlet fever in June 1893. Jennie was expecting her second child when Margaret died. She gave birth to Edmund later in the year. Two more children were born after Edmund, Thomas and Helen.

The silver strikes made Jennie and Tom very wealthy. They decided to move to Salt Lake City. They had a large house built for their family on Brigham Street, near the home of Brigham Young, the leader of the Mormon congregation. The family moved into this home in 1901. Tom was interested in local politics. He gained the respect of many people in Salt Lake City. He was already well known due to the success of the silver mines. Tom decided to run for a seat in the U.S. Senate. He won the election and served for four years. After this, Tom returned to running the mining companies. He and David Keith bought the *Salt Lake City Tribune* newspaper. The two men ran the newspaper for a few years, then turned the management over to other family members.

Meanwhile, Jennie was tending to her children. She made sure they went to school and church. When her stepsister Francis died, leaving a five year old son, Jennie took him into her home. This boy, Jack Gallagher, became another one of her children. Jennie cared deeply about children who did not have loving parents to care for them. She was instrumental in having the Kearns-Saint Ann's Orphanage built in Salt Lake City. She donated $55,000 to the Catholic Bishop, Lawrence Scanlon, so that he could buy the land for the orphanage. She supplied funds so that the children living in the orphanage could have dance and music lessons. Every year at Christmastime, she hosted a holiday party in her home for all of the children who lived in the orphanage. Jennie also gave generously during the fundraising drive to have the Cathedral of the Madeleine built in Salt Lake City.

In 1918, Tom was struck by a car while walking to his house. He suffered a stroke following the collision. Tom lingered for a few days, then passed away from his injuries. Jennie mourned Tom's passing, wearing only black clothing for many years. She was left with a fortune estimated to be many millions of dollars. Jennie gave away thousands of dollars of this fortune to worthy causes. People heard her say, "You know, it's just no good to have lots of money if you can't do good things with it."

After Tom's death, Jennie became the president of the Kearns Corporation which dealt in investments, mining, real estate and other ventures. She became the owner of the *Salt Lake Tribune-Telegram Publishing Company.* She managed her family's finances until the end of her life. In 1937, Jennie donated her home in Salt Lake City to the city. The house became the governor's residence for many years. Jennie kept a house in Reno, Nevada. She also went to stay with her children in their homes. She enjoyed being with her grandchildren. Her son Edmund passed away in 1936. Her daughter Helen passed away a few years later in 1943 while she was visiting Jennie in her Reno home. Jennie passed away only a few months later on September 23, 1943. She was visiting a cousin in San Francisco, California at the time of her death.

In some ways, Jennie's life was like that of many other women of the time. She supported her husband in his business and political interests but did not seek publicity for herself. She did use her influence to ensure that the wealth that came to Tom and herself was directed in ways that benefited others, especially children. She became a savvy business woman when that role was bequeathed to her. Jennie was well respected for being judicious when she came to be in charge of millions of dollars. More so than being a fiscally responsible businessperson, Jennie is remembered for her generosity in sharing her wealth.

VERMONT:
Wealth in Character

Hannah Malan McCarty

Hannah McCarty was born in the year 1824 in County Cork, Ireland. She was the daughter of John and Hannah Murphy Malan. She and her husband James McCarty emigrated from Ireland in 1850, five years after the potato famine began. They settled in Northfield, Vermont. During the next twenty years, eight children were born into their family. James worked as a laborer but did not own any land. His personal property consisted of $100. James died in 1871, two days after his youngest child was born.

Hannah was left to raise the children. As soon as her children were old enough, they all found jobs. Her sons worked on railroad crews. Her daughters worked in local restaurants and as domestic servants. The family stayed together by pooling their wages every week.

Many citizens of Northfield, during the mid 19th century, harbored feelings of dislike and distrust of immigrants settling in the village. Irish immigrants, non-native and usually Catholic, received a great deal of criticism. One of the local newspapers ran an article labeling the Irish immigrants as a "foreign, aggressive, and uncongenial element." The immigrants who spoke the Irish language rather than the English language were scorned and mocked. Some people believed the Catholics' loyalty to the Catholic teachings and the Pope in Rome would take precedence over the ideals of American democracy as they defined it. These discriminatory feelings grew into a political party called the 'Know-Nothings'. In 1855, nearly 400 delegates of the party held a convention in Northfield.

The anti-Irish sentiment in Northfield made it difficult for many workers, like Hannah's children, to work in any capacity that would allow them to attain a more comfortable standard of living. It was not until 1885, fourteen years after James's death, that Hannah and her children were able to own a house of their own without a mortgage attached. The house was located on Water Street near the Dog River which passed through the village.

None of Hannah's sons married. All of them remained with Hannah at the home they purchased in 1885. Hannah lived in that house for the remainder of her life. During those years, all of her sons died. One son, Charles, who worked for the Vermont Central Railroad as a freight conductor, died at the age of forty-six. Another son, Thomas, was forty-five years old when he passed away from tuberculosis. John died at the age of forty-five after falling from a carriage. Hannah's other two sons also died at relatively young ages. Her daughter Katherine remained at home throughout her life as well. Katherine died from colitis at the age of sixty-one years. Ellen passed away at home as well when she was twenty-six years old. Mary was Hannah's only child to marry. She married James E. Meagher, a plumber in Burlington, Vermont in 1901. Hannah hosted the wedding party in her home, where she provided the wedding breakfast. Mary and James did not have children. Mary passed away suddenly in 1946 when she was seventy-five years old.

Hannah lived to be ninety-eight years old. She lived longer than all of her children but one. She died around August 25, 1922. The *Northfield News* newspaper mentioned in her obituary that "her years of struggle" were now finished. There are many stories of Irish immigrants who found, after years of hard work and sacrifice, wealth and respected positions in the communities where they settled. There are also many stories of Irish immigrants who did not realize the 'American Dream' of riches and status they had heard about before immigrating to America. Hannah's

life story more closely resembles the latter. Yet, in her obituary, she was praised as a "woman of wonderful vitality...She was a friend to every child in her neighborhood. Until the last she retained a remarkable memory and was probably more familiar with Northfield's early history than any other citizen." There were people around Hannah who found much to admire in her character. They admired her perseverance and loyalty and friendliness. Her character was her wealth.

"Celtic Cross" Public Domain Image

VIRGINIA:
A Life Fulfilled

Pauline Forstall Colclough Adams

"Mrs. Pauline Adams in the prison garb she wore while serving a sixty-day sentence." Created between 1917 September and 1919 February 15. Women of Protest: National Woman's Party Records, Group 1, Container 1:147, folder, Adams, Pauline Library of Congress Prints and Photographs Division

Pauline Forstall Colclough was born in Dublin, Ireland on June 29, 1874. Her parents were Henry Vesey and Margaret Forstall Colclough. Pauline was the third child in the family. She had two older sisters, Angeline and Constance. One younger brother, John, completed the family. The entire Colclough family immigrated to the United States aboard the ship *Wyoming* in 1883. They sailed from Liverpool, England and landed in New York City. Nine year old Pauline was very excited to arrive in a new city and a new country. The family did not remain in New York. They made their way to Brunswick County, North Carolina and settled there. Pauline married Doctor Walter J. Adams in 1898. They moved to Norfolk, Virginia where Walter had previously been living. Walter wanted to establish his medical practice in Norfolk. One year later, Pauline gave birth to a son, Walter Paul Adams. Her second son, Edward Forstall Adams was born in 1902.

By the year 1910, Pauline's children were both occupied with school and lessons. Pauline had some time in the day for her own interests. She hosted a meeting in her home which led to the formation of the Norfolk Equal Suffrage League. The women at the meeting voted for Pauline to be their first president. Pauline did not think trying to educate people on women's suffrage by giving lectures was the best method of gaining support for the cause. She advocated marching in the street, carrying banners and disrupting official ceremonies. Some of the suffragettes supported Pauline's methods, while others condemned these actions. In 1913, Pauline, along with two other women from Virginia, attended a women's suffrage conference in Washington, D.C. 300 women attended the conference. The members marched in the national suffrage parade held in the city the day before Woodrow Wilson was inaugurated as the U.S. President.

Pauline joined the Congressional Union for Woman Suffrage in 1917. She was named president of the group which was renamed the National Woman's Party. Pauline served as president of the party from 1917-1920. During World War I, the women continued to advocate for equal suffrage. Pauline campaigned for a women's home guard to be instituted in Norfolk. She and her fellow members sold war bonds and stamps in the city. The women picketed outside the White House, holding banners that read, "Mr. President, how long must women wait for liberty?" The women proclaimed that if the United States government would fight for democracy across the ocean in Europe, then the government must support democracy by way of equal suffrage at home in the United States. Thirteen members held banners and picketed in front of President Wilson's reviewing stand during a military parade on September 4, 1917. The women were arrested and given a choice between $25 fines for each or sixty days in prison. All of the women chose to go to prison. Pauline and the others were sent to a women's workhouse at Occoquan, Fairfax County, Virginia. Pauline was placed in solitary confinement. She was not given a blanket, nor a toothbrush or hairbrush for the duration. When the women were released from prison on November 4, 1917, they reported that they had been cut off from contact with the world outside the prison. Pauline told of the worm-infested food the women had been fed or forced to consume. Pauline recounted the difficult conditions which the women and the others in the prison experienced in a letter she wrote to her son Walter.

In L.D.C. Jail

Dearest Walter,

"Hope everything is all right with you and the home bunch
but I have been kept from the privilege of in coming or
outgoing mail for over the past week and am now located
in a small cell in "solitary". I have not been given my tooth
brush or hair-brush here yet but got the loan of this pencil
from a new picket who came with another group yesterday.
Two leave tomorrow. They only got 30 days while others
have 6 Months for doing the same thing "blocking traffic"
which is the false charge they trump up against us. There
was no one crowding around when I was arrested.

Just ten days from tomorrow....write Miss Crocker
and tell home news as well as whether you can come
down. I am sure the rest and change from my house
keeping to Elizabeth's has done Dad and family good.

Good bye

Your loving

Mother"

After Pauline's release from prison, she fervently supported prison reform.
In 1918, Pauline and all of the other women picketers who were arrested
won the case brought before the District of Columbia Appeals Court.
The Court ruled that all of the women had been illegally arrested and
imprisoned. Pauline and the other women who had been imprisoned
toured the country encouraging the women they met to support the
suffrage movement. Pauline was one of 166 women who was given a 'prison
pin' in 1920 to commemorate their sacrifices for the cause of suffrage.

The 19th Amendment legalizing women's right to vote was passed in
August 1920. Pauline, now forty-six years old, took up another challenge.
She undertook the bar examination in 1921 which she passed successfully.
She was now able to practice law, becoming among the first women in

Virginia to do so and only the second woman in Norfolk to hold such a license. She advocated for women in legal matters where previously they had little say or support from many who worked in the legal system. She continued participating in politics. She unsuccessfully ran for a seat on the Norfolk City Council. She turned her energies to assisting another woman, Sarah Lee Fain, who was campaigning to become a member of the Virginia House of Delegates. Sarah Lee was elected as a delegate in 1923.

During Pauline's later years, she and Walter traveled to many other countries. Pauline was interested to learn about the rights of women in other countries. She continued to champion causes that promoted women's equality. Walter passed away in 1939. Pauline continued to live in Norfolk. Her son Walter became a doctor like his father. He served in the United States Navy during World War II. Her son Edward served in the military as well and excelled as a mathematician. When Pauline passed away on September 10, 1957, she was buried next to Walter in Elmwood Cemetery, in Norfolk City. The inscription on Pauline's gravestone reads, "A Life Fulfilled".

WASHINGTON:
Friend and Mother to All

Teresa Lappin Eldridge

Teresa Lappin was born in Derryhale, County Armagh, Ireland on June 24, 1832. Her parents were Alexander and Elizabeth Hughes Lappin. When Teresa was eighteen years old, she and one of her sisters immigrated to New York City. They found work as domestic servants with a family living on Long Island, New York. After working for the family for one

year, the sisters joined a ship full of single women traveling together to the new state of California. The women were answering a call for women to come to California to help build the population of the state. The ship sailed through the Isthmus of Panama on its way to San Francisco.

One of the crew onboard the ship was a man named Edward Eldridge. Edward was born in St. Andrews, Fifeshire, Scotland on December 7, 1829. At a very young age, he had run away to a life on the sea. He sailed to America, landing in New York in 1846. From there, he made his way to Michigan where he took a job crewing on ships on the Great Lakes. He returned to ocean sailing after a while. When the ship

"Teresa Lapin Eldridge" Catalog No. X.5000.2
Studio portrait of Teresa Lapin Eldridge
Courtesy Whatcom Museum of History & Art,
Bellingham, Washington

he was on sailed into the port at San Francisco, Edward departed. He found another job on the steamer ship, the *Tennessee*. This was one of the mailboats owned by the Pacific Mail Steamship Company. In addition to carrying mail between San Francisco and Panama, these mailboats also ferried travelers from the United States to the California Territory. The ships were used by thousands of men trying to get to California once gold was discovered there. The *Tennessee* was the ship Teresa Lappin and the other women were booked on to sail to San Francisco.

Teresa and Edward met onboard the ship. During the journey, which took three weeks, they decided to marry. Their wedding took place soon after they arrived in San Francisco. Edward resigned from the Pacific Mail Line in order to prospect for gold in California. He did not find any gold but he did meet a ship captain that he had known during his time on the Great Lakes. The man was Captain Henry Roeder. Captain Roeder had retired from shipping and taken up mining. He turned his back on mining when he learned about the vast forests in the northern Washington Territory around Bellingham Bay. He and a partner planned to build a lumber mill on a site at What-Coom Falls. Captain Roeder encouraged Edward to join him in this endeavor.

Edward accepted the captain's offer. In 1853, Edward, Teresa and their infant daughter, Isabelle, made the journey to Bellingham Bay on a schooner Captain Roeder chartered. An additional eight men joined the group. The journey took many days, but finally, the anchor was dropped in an estuary below What-Coom Creek Falls. Teresa held Isabelle in her arms while she was carried from the schooner to the shore. Mother and daughter were the first non-indigenous women to come to the settlement which came to be called Whatcom. Their first home was near the site where Captain Roeder built a sawmill.

The men at the mill site set to work to build a cabin suitable for Teresa and Isabelle. The cabin was made of logs cut from the nearby forest. After the cabin was finished, the men set to work setting up the machines and equipment Captain Roeder had brought with him for the sawmill. They also built a bunkhouse for themselves. They built bunks, benches, tables and cupboards for the Eldridge family.

As the lone woman at the lumber mill, the job of feeding all of the mill workers fell to Teresa and occupied nearly all of her time. It was expected that she would prepare three hot meals each day for the men. Thanks to the generosity of the local indigenous women living nearby, Teresa was able to carry out her duties as the camp cook. The women brought gifts of berries and fish and other foods to her each morning. The food was a welcome addition to the meager supplies Teresa had available. The women also took Isabelle with them for the day, watching over her. Isabelle spent the days in the woods or at the water's edge while the women picked berries or fished. She was lovingly cared for and learned her first words in the women's language.

Teresa and Edward claimed 320 acres of land in 1854 under the Donation Land Claim Act. One of the requirements for eventually owning the land was that the claimant(s) had to live on the land for four consecutive years. After Edward built a cabin, the family moved to this location. The land was not good for growing crops, however. Edward began thinking about prospecting again. He had heard about gold strikes in the Okanogan Region east of newly organized Whatcom County. Edward left Teresa, now expecting a baby, and Isabelle on their claim. In his absence, Edward was elected to the Territorial Legislature for Whatcom County. When he learned of this, Edward traveled to the Territorial capital at Olympia. He remained in Olympia for two legislative sessions. Teresa gave birth to her son Edward on May 10, 1855 while her husband Edward was away.

Teresa recalled later in her life, the time when she managed the Eldridge Claim, her two young children, and the cooking duties of the camp at the mill. "We depended almost entirely on the Lummi Indians for food...They brought us clams, fish, and many different sorts of birds', ducks', gulls' and divers' eggs."

When Edward returned, he decided that farming was not going to provide the family with a living. Edward joined the men working in the newly opened Sehome Coal Mine. The family moved to be closer to the mine. Teresa opened a boarding house for the miners coming into the area. The boarding house was a great success and eventually grew to become the Keystone Hotel. Teresa gave birth to another child, Alice and then a son, Hugh.

The next move for the family came about in 1862. They moved into a large house at a location known as the Squalicum Creek Farm. By this time, Edward was very well known throughout the settlement, the county and the entire Territory. Teresa found herself preparing meals and setting her table, on some days, multiple times, as people passing through the area came to see Edward. She hosted politicians, dignitaries, academics and pioneer settlers. She was at ease with all of her visitors. It was said of her that she made everyone who came into her house feel welcomed.

Tragedy struck when thirteen year old Edward was accidentally shot and killed in 1868 while in a boat on the bay. Teresa and Edward were filled with grief. Teresa carried on, raising her other three children and serving the growing community. Edward was selected to be a delegate to the Territorial Constitutional Convention in 1878. He served as a delegate to the State Constitutional Convention as well. Teresa and Edward were pleased to see Washington admitted into the Union on November 11, 1889.

Alice Eldridge, married in 1878 to James Gilliam, passed away in 1886 at the age of twenty-eight, leaving three young children. Teresa helped to raise her grandchildren. Edward passed away on October 13, 1892. At the time of his death, he held a great number of leadership and political positions in the town and in Whatcom County. Shortly after these sad events, Teresa watched as the family's mansion burned to the ground during a forest fire which raged through the town and beyond in 1894. One bright spot during this time was the marriage of her son Hugh to Delesea J. Bowers in 1893. Hugh was the postmaster in Whatcom for many years.

Teresa continued living in Whatcom which was renamed Bellingham. The town name was changed in 1903 when the towns on the bay consolidated. Teresa came to be known as the 'Mother of Whatcom' due to her early arrival in the original settlement and her caring nature. From the moment she had been carried ashore many years ago, Teresa's care and generosity toward others was present at all times. When she passed away on May 10, 1911, the entire town mourned. On the day of her funeral, shops were closed and business suspended for the day. The mayor of Bellingham declared that the flag over the city hall would be flown at half mast. Thousands of people living in the town and neighboring areas lined the streets to respectfully watch the funeral cortège pass. Teresa's obituary stated that all of the decorum and respect shown at her funeral was a testimony to "the passing of the pioneer woman and mother of Bellingham Bay by the people who are now living to take her place."

WASHINGTON, D.C.:

The Explosion

Bridget Dunn and the Women of the Washington Arsenal Explosion

The outside temperature reached nearly 100 degrees Farenheit in the town of Washington, District of Columbia on June 17, 1864. Inside the Washington Arsenal Factory, women and girls were making munitions. The workers in the arsenals, both men and women, while not on the front lines of battles ongoing during the U.S. Civil War, were an important, necessary component to the war effort for the opposing sides. In addition to the women working in the arsenal in Washington D.C., other women worked in the arsenal in the Union city of Pittsburgh, Pennsylvania. Women arsenal workers were found in the Confederate cities of Richmond, Virginia and Augusta, Georgia. 110 women and young girls were employed in the Washington arsenal. Some of the women packed munitions into boxes which were then sent to Union camps. Thirty women spent their working hours in the choking room. It was their job to pack cartridges with gunpowder. Next, a bullet was inserted, then the cartridge was tied off, or choked by use of a machine. The finished cartridges were packed in boxes. Women were hired for this work because it was believed that the work suited a woman's smaller hands and that women had better fine motor skills for working with the cartridges.

Many of the women who worked in the arsenal were Irish immigrants or daughters born to recent Irish immigrants. Most of the women were barely past their teenage years. Some of them were only twelve or thirteen years old. Many lived at home with their families. Their earnings from the arsenal work helped to support their families. Some married women worked in the arsenal because they were their family's main financial support. On this June day, the women filed into work as usual. They were all wearing hooped skirts and long-sleeved blouses in spite of the hot summer temperatures. Their clothing was meant to keep them well covered and to discourage any distraction from work the men in the arsenal might face from having women as co-workers. Before settling into the work shift, one of the officials in the factory read aloud a letter which thanked the workers for their recent monetary contribution of $170 for a monument which was being designed to commemorate the 78 victims of an explosion at the Pittsburgh Arsenal. The explosion had occurred two years earlier. Many of those victims were women and girls, just like the workers at the Washington Arsenal.

Afterwards, the women settled into their work. There was Bridget Dunn who had emigrated from County Wexford, Ireland. She was born in 1819, making her one of the older women employees. Bridget was not married. She had a room in a boarding house at 32 East Capitol Street. Another employee was Ellen Roche. She was eighteen years old and the eldest of eight siblings. Her income supplemented the money her father earned as a laborer and her mother earned as a washerwoman. Johanna Connor and Margaret Horgan were there, as well as Elizabeth Branagan, Emily Collins and Kate Brosnahan.

The air inside the choking room soon became stifling. A window was opened to allow for any breeze. One of the women was laughing and chatting while at her work station. A supervisor immediately dismissed her because chatting during work was against the rules. As she left the room, she complained of her misfortune to another woman. Her friend tried to console her by telling her that maybe it was for the best. Back at the long table, running east to west through the room, the women sat on benches on both sides. All was quiet as everyone got on with their work. One of the women sitting on the south side of a bench was Bridget Dunn.

Unbeknownst to Bridget and the other women, the superintendent of the arsenal, Thomas Brown, had placed outside, near their building, some flares in the shape of stars. He had made the stars that morning for use in lighting the night sky and for the upcoming July 4th celebrations. Thomas was a pyrotechnic expert. He had worked in the arsenal for over twenty years. It was against safety rules to have any sulfur in the mix for these flares so Thomas used his own recipe to make the incendiaries. After he constructed the flares, he set them outside in copper pans to dry in the sun. The pans were located about 30-35 feet away from where the women were working. As the outside temperature climbed that morning, the copper pans absorbed heat. The heat led to the flares igniting. As the flares began to pop, one of them sailed through the open window of the choking room. The time was just before noon.

Working with gunpowder in the choking room meant that there were always remnants of gunpowder dust, or residue on the long table where the women sat. The flare hit the table, igniting sparks from the gunpowder it met. The sparks ignited more of the gunpowder which led to small fires racing down the table. At one end of the table, a barrel containing gunpowder then ignited and exploded. Fire was everywhere. All of the women at the table were holding cartridges which had the ball of the cartridge pointing at them. As the fire spread, the cartridges discharged into the women. There was instant chaos as the women screamed in pain and fear and tried to get away from the fire. They were hampered by the cumbersome hoops in their skirts. The women sitting on the north side of the table had a better opportunity since they were closer to the doors leading from the room. The women sitting on the south side of the table had no chance at all. Bridget Dunn was sitting on the south side of the table. Next to her sat Julia McKewen and Kate Horgan. Some of the others on that side of the table were Maggie Yonson, Margaret Tippett, Johanna Connor and Ellen Roche. Across from Bridget sat Kate Bresnahan, Miss Lloyd, Florence Kennedy and others. Most likely, each of the women had about 500 cartridges in front of her.

Edward Stebbins, the paymaster at the arsenal, saw 'something' fly through the air when the explosions began. He raced to the building and threw open the doors. He was able to help about forty women escape outside. The clothing of many of the women was on fire and many of the women were badly burned. Mr. Stebbins did not think that any of the women sitting on the south side of the table could have gotten themselves out from their seats before fire consumed them.

When the fires were finally extinguished, rescuers entered the burnt building. They found only body parts and charred remains inside of wire hoops. Very few of the bodies could be named. The roll call books and log books of employees were lost in the fire. Crowds of people raced to the factory gates. An order was issued to not allow onlookers inside. Relatives were anxious for news of their wives, daughters, sisters and children. When the injured women who had been taken to the hospital or taken home were accounted for, those left and presumed dead were named. The *Evening Star Newspaper* listed the women: Bridget Dunn, East Capitol street, supposed to be killed. Ellen Roche, also supposed to be killed. A total of 21 women were subsequently named as victims of the explosion. Some of the bodies were so badly burned, they could not be identified with assurance. A few of the women were identified by remnants of clothing or jewelry that clung to them. Johanna Connor, who lived on English Hill, was among those only recognized by a portion of dress which remained upon her. But for the fragment of dress it would have been impossible to recognize her.

Funerals for the women began the next day. Some of the women were buried in the Catholic Cemetery. Bridget Dunn's funeral was conducted on June 19th in the house where she had lived. Many people joined her funeral procession with at least twenty carriages. Some of her neighbors acted as pallbearers. She was buried in Mt. Oliver Cemetery located in the town. A mass funeral for most of the victims took place on the grounds of the arsenal. The funeral cortège was meant to leave the grounds at 3:00 P.M., on June 19. People began arriving long before the starting time. By 2:00 P.M., there were over 1,000 people waiting at the gate to the factory. When the gates opened at 2:30 P.M., there were several thousand in attendance.

There were 15 coffins underneath a canopy. Eight of the coffins were marked with the name 'unknown'. Seven bore a plate with the woman's name upon it. All of the coffins were decorated with bouquets and wreaths. Ministers of various faiths conducted the service together. Father Bokel came from St. Dominick's Catholic Church. Reverend Leech came from the Methodist Episcopal Church. After the service was concluded, a long line, beginning with the pallbearers, led the procession from the arsenal. Next in line following them was President Abraham Lincoln and the Secretary of War, Edwin Stanton. President Lincoln was not in attendance as a speaker that day. He came only as another mourner of lives lost in service to their country. Edwin Stanton sent a note to the commandant of the arsenal, Major Benton, that all "funeral expenses incident to the internment of the sufferers by the recent catastrophe at the Arsenal will be paid by the Department. You will not spare any means to express the respect and sympathy of the Government for the deceased and their surviving friends." The coffins were taken to the Congressional Cemetery and buried all together.

An inquest into the cause of the explosion and fire was held after the funerals. There were so many witnesses, the judge called a halt to having them come forward. It was agreed that Thomas Brown had been negligent by placing the star flares to dry too close to a building where people were inside working with explosives. He was to be severely reprimanded but no criminal charges were made.

The Washington Arsenal employees and the families and neighbors of the dead women wanted a monument erected to commemorate them. They began collecting money in order to commission the monument. One year later, they had collected $3,000. Flannery Brothers Marble Manufacturers was hired to build the monument. Lot Flannery was selected as the sculptor. He designed a monument reaching 25 feet in height. Atop the monument, a young girl looks downward in sadness. The monument was titled, "Grief". The names of the women who died in the explosion were then carved into the stone.

Bridget Dunn gave her life in service to her country along with twenty other women that day. Age has never been a prerequisite for brave acts as exemplified by Bridget, who at age forty-five, might have been thought too old to be engaged in war work. She and her deceased work sisters, most only twenty years of age, and one, only twelve years, went into the arsenal factory every working day, knowing the risks yet hoping for the best. It is fitting that they be remembered as veterans and heroes.

"Arsenal Explosion Monument" Creator: Fraser, Clayton B. 2004.
Library of Congress Prints and Photographs Division HALS DC-1-35

WEST VIRGINIA:
The Agitator

Mary Harris "Mother" Jones

Mary Harris was born in Cork City, County Cork, Ireland. Her exact birthday is unknown but her baptismal date was August 1, 1837. Her father was Richard Harris, a tenant farmer, and her mother was Ellen Cotter Harris. The family farmed land in the rural village of Inchigeelagh. Potatoes were their staple crop. Like thousands of other Irish people, the Harris Family fell victim to the starvation and poverty the potato famine in Ireland wrought beginning in 1845. In 1847 when there were no potatoes left to eat, Mary's father and one brother left Cork for America. They found work on a railroad building crew which took them to Toronto, Canada. They settled in Toronto. Mary, her mother and the rest of the family immigrated to the United States a few years later, after Richard and Mary's brother had saved enough money to pay for their passage on a ship. The ship sailed into Boston Harbor in 1850. From there, the family made their way to Toronto. Everyone was delighted to be reunited. The children were enrolled in school. Mary continued her education at the Toronto Normal School after she finished in the local school. She received her qualification to teach school. In 1859, when she was twenty-two years old, Mary accepted a teaching position in the town of Monroe, Michigan.

Teaching in a classroom did not fulfill Mary. After a few months, she left Michigan for Chicago, Illinois. She had been trained in needlework while in Toronto which led to her becoming a fine seamstress. She found work as a dressmaker. She stayed in Chicago for a few months. Then she relocated to Memphis, Tennessee. Once again, Mary accepted a teaching position. While living in Memphis, Mary became acquainted with a man named George Jones. George worked for the Union Iron Works in Memphis as an iron molder. This was a skilled position which paid well. In 1861, Mary and George decided to marry. Mary left her teaching position in order to keep house and to care for the children that soon joined their family. Four children were born between 1862-1867. They were Catherine, Elizabeth, Terrence and Mary.

The year 1867 was one of economic and personal tragedies for Mary. Rising unemployment in the ironworks after the U.S. Civil War led to job cuts and decreased wages for the workers who held onto their jobs. During the summer months, a yellow fever epidemic swept through the city. All of Mary and George's children were victims of the disease. After the children's deaths, George succumbed as well. Mary was left alone to grieve the loss of her entire family. The union workers at the iron works company took up a collection for Mary. Mary, in turn, began to assist in the care of other yellow fever victims. She was not a trained nurse, but did what she could to help other victims. Sometimes, she was only able to offer palliative care and comfort.

When the epidemic ended, Mary decided that it was time for her to move away from Memphis. She returned to Chicago once again. This time, Mary opened her own dress shop. Her business was a success. Many of her clients were affluent citizens of the city. At times, when Mary was sewing a dress for a client, she glanced outside her shop windows. She noticed the poor people walking along the shore of Lake Michigan, dressed in tattered clothes and worn shoes. She thought about the disparity between her clients and these people.

In 1871, a great fire roared through the city of Chicago. The fire claimed Mary's shop and all of her inventory, as well as her house and all of her worldly goods. She was left with nothing and no one again. Mary and many others did what they could to help rebuild the city. It was during these days that Mary became invested in the plight of workers who had no one to speak for them. In numerous industries and trades, workers worked very long shifts and were inadequately compensated. Mary was particularly opposed to child labor practices. In her autobiography, written years later, Mary stated that thinking about her own husband, a staunch supporter of unions, and her children, drove her to be passionate about workers' rights. She had not been able to save her children or her husband, but she could stand against poverty and oppression in the workplace and thus, hopefully, help to facilitate better lives for working people.

In 1893, the United States entered into an economic depression. Many people were left without jobs. Without income, many lost their homes. A man named Jacob Conley organized unemployed men for a march to Washington D.C. The marchers planned to call for the creation of a federal jobs program. Mary worked as a volunteer, encouraging men to march. She walked with the marchers to Washington D.C. She helped to procure food and transportation for the men. The march was covered by news media throughout the country. Other organizers began planning strikes to demand action for the unemployed. 125,000 United Mine Workers went on strike the next year. The American Railway Union went on strike. Mary encouraged strikes for better working conditions, better pay, health benefits and child protection laws all over the United States. She was particularly interested in the plight of coal miners in West Virginia because the corporate owners of the mines seemed to control every part of a worker's life.

Mary was encouraging these miners to join the United Mine Workers. She

"Mother Jones" Creator: Howell, Bertha, photographer, published 1902. Library of Congress Prints and Photographs Division LC-DIG-ds-07711

organized food deliveries to striking miners in western Pennsylvania. She encouraged women to join the strikers as well. In Anthracite City, in eastern Pennsylvania, Mary organized strikers' wives to prevent non-union workers from entering the mines during a strike. Groups of women known as the 'broom and mop' brigades kept guard at the entrances to mines. Mary was tireless in her efforts to keep the strike on until, finally, President Theodore Roosevelt ordered the owner of the anthracite mine, J.P. Morgan, to attend an arbitration meeting which included union members.

As the 20th century dawned, Mary returned to West Virginia. She was committed to helping the miners there gain a foothold against the corporation owners. In 1902, during one strike, police arrested many of the strikers. Mary was arrested as well.

During her trial, the district attorney labeled Mary, "the most dangerous woman in America." Mary received a suspended sentence while most of the strike leaders were put in prison. The judge reasoned that if he sent Mary to prison, her followers would consider her a martyr for the cause which would lead to more men joining the union.

Mary did not let the strikers' defeat in West Virginia stop her. She told people, "My address is like my shoes. It travels with me. I abide where there is a fight against wrong." She set out for Colorado where she would again encourage miners to join the United Mine Workers. Similarly to the mines in West Virginia, the Colorado mines were owned by corporations who ruled over nearly every aspect of their workers' lives. When a referendum supporting an eight hour work day for miners passed, it was never put into practice because the Colorado Legislature would not go against the powerful corporations.

From Colorado, Mary traveled to Philadelphia to organize a children's march which would travel to President Theodore Roosevelt's summer home in New York. Her plan was to expose the horrors of child labor in factories. Over 200 children marched. Many of the children were victims of injuries by machinery. Many of them worked sixty hours weekly and did not attend school. The strike was not successful in obtaining shorter working hours and the cessation of night work for women and children but it was a first step in bringing attention to the cause of child labor.

Mary continued her travels in the name of workers' rights. She traveled to Mexico to stand up for workers there as well. In 1911, Mary was hired by the United Mine Workers to travel to West Virginia once again to rally miners there. Since these miners received very little pay, West Virginia coal could be bought cheaply. This made West Virginia coal very attractive to buyers. The mine owners had no interest in listening to claims from workers about their working conditions. The owners were not interested in negotiating with the miners either. Violence was their usual retaliatory gesture when talk of miners unionizing arose. Two of the mines, one in Cabin Creek and one in Paint Creek, were isolated from towns. Punishments by the mine owners' guards were often not reported.

In 1912, Mary, now known as 'Mother', spoke at a rally in the town of Eskdale, West Virginia. Eskdale was one of only a few towns not controlled by corporate mine owners. People could meet in the town to discuss unionizing. Mary used her powerful voice to encourage the workers into signing on as union members. A number of the miners decided to strike in August. The West Virginia Governor, Glasscock, declared martial law in September of 1912. The governor sent in military troops who took away the strikers' weapons but left machine guns with the mine owners. Many of the strikers were arrested, including Mother Jones. She was confined for three months in prison. All of those arrested faced court martial.

When Mother Jones went into the courtroom for her trial, she was seventy-six years old and in poor health. The judge at her trial sentenced her to twenty years in prison. News of her confinement and trial was widely covered and discussed all across the country. Officials in West Virginia were besieged with protest letters and criticism of their actions against her. During her incarceration at Mrs. Carney's Boarding House, Mother Jones developed a dangerous case of pneumonia. Eventually, the state of West Virginia agreed to some of the miners' demands. The miners were granted a nine hour workday. The deplorable conditions in the mines were exposed during a United States Senate Commission. The mine owners were forced to recognize the union in Cabin Creek and Paint Creek. Mother Jones became even more well known after her release from prison.

Advancing in age did not slow Mother Jones. She traveled to Ludlow, Colorado where miners were living in horrific conditions. In spite of her campaigns there, the owners won and the debilitated miners had to return to work without making any gains. Failure only spurred Mother Jones on. She traveled on behalf of garment workers in Chicago and streetcar workers in another part of Illinois. In 1917, she returned once again to West Virginia. Coal was commanding a higher price now that countries were at war. The miners in West Virginia thought that, at last, better working conditions might be possible since they were sorely needed to keep the coal in ready supply. The miners were not allowed to strike during war time, but Mother Jones did not think the 'no strike' law should be obeyed. She was dismayed at the living conditions of the miners. They had no access to health care and their homes were little more than huts.

The next time Mother Jones came to West Virginia was in 1921. She was unsuccessful at deterring the miners from staging a march which became known as the 'March on Logan'. When the marchers were imprisoned, Mother Jones visited the Governor, Ephraim Franklin Morgan, petitioning him to pardon the miners. Mother Jones was now nearly ninety years old. Her body was slowing down, though her mind was sharp. She was plagued with rheumatism and no longer able to travel easily. She went to stay with friends living in Washington, D.C. In 1924, she wrote her autobiography. She claimed to have been born in 1830 which led to even more accolades for all of her work on behalf of unrepresented workers.

On May 1, 1930, Mother Jones celebrated her 100th birthday. She passed away a few months later on November 30, 1930. She was buried in the Miners Cemetery in Mount Olive, Illinois. Representatives of different unions carried her casket to its resting place. The music for her funeral Mass was sung by a choir composed of miners. Mary Harris, Mother Jones, said to many workers in her lifetime, "Pray for the dead and fight like hell for the living."

WISCONSIN:
How Ever Far We Roam

Anna Emily Cook Gogin and Her Daughters

Anna Emily Cook was born in 1832 in County Cork, Ireland. She immigrated with family members to the United States where she came to live in Philadelphia, Pennsylvania. In 1855, Anna and Richard Gogin, also from County Cork, married. One year later, they left Philadelphia with their newborn baby girl, Mary, in a covered wagon, pulled by oxen. They headed west to Wisconsin where Richard planned to buy land for farming. Their first home was in the town of Leon, Waushara County, Wisconsin.

While Richard set about clearing land and putting in their first crops, Anna established their home and cared for Mary. In 1858, another daughter, Anna Elizabeth, was born. In 1861 and 1863, Richard and James were born. During this time, the U.S. Civil War was ongoing. Richard joined Company B of the 16th Wisconsin Volunteers in February 1864. He was away from home until he was mustered out in July 1865 after the war had ended. Richard made his way back to Wisconsin where his family and farm awaited him. Anna had kept their home and farm going while caring for her four young children. The following year, 1866, another child was born. Anna and Richard named him John Sherman, in an homage to General Sherman of the Union Army. Ella Gogin was born in 1868, then Gertrude in 1870, George in 1872, Arthur in 1875 and Mabel in 1878. All of the children attended the rural school located near the family home. Some of the children were taught by their own older sisters after they had qualified to become teachers.

Mary Gogin, known as Mollie to her family, was one of the teachers in the school. Her younger brother John was one of her students. John wrote in a letter to Mollie, possibly an assignment Mollie gave to her pupils, that, "For my part I am well satisfied onelly that you have been a little to easy with us sometimes." Mollie's sister Ann, twenty-two years old in 1880, was married and the mother of two children. One son, George, had only lived for two years. Everyone else was still living at home. By the next year, however, the children began setting out to make their own way in the world. All five daughters taught in rural schools at some point in their young lives.

In September, Anna's daughter Mollie left to take a teaching position away from the Leon, Wisconsin school. She received a letter from her sister Ella in December. Ella, who was thirteen years old now, had taken the teaching position in the Leon school. Among her students were her younger siblings, Arthur and Mabel, six and four years old. Ella wrote in her letter that "I have a splendid school this Winter and it hardly seems possible that it's so near out." Ella also wrote that she was not happy about the behavior of two of the students. Her concerns were for her own brother and sister! In her classroom, Ella also taught students older than herself. One of her students was nineteen years old.

Ella wrote to Mollie again in July 1882. She reported that she was the eldest child in the home now. Anna was still mostly occupied with caring for her youngest children. Ella wrote that her mother did have time for a few outings. Anna and Richard sometimes visited the men in the Soldier's Home, a place for veterans who had nowhere else to live. She also let Mollie know that she was working to achieve an endorsement to her teaching license. She paid attention to what the local people said and thought about the school. She attended the school board meetings. During one meeting, those in attendance voted on whether the school district or the students' families should purchase the books needed during school terms. A measure was passed to have the students procure their own textbooks. Those who voted in favor of the measure then decided that since students would henceforth buy their own books, the books already in the school could be sold at auction. No one bid on the books so Ella bought the entire lot for $2.21. She realized that students would either buy new books or, for slightly less money, buy these same books back from her. Ella made a tidy profit when parents returned the next day to the school in order to purchase textbooks.

Mollie Gogin was teaching in a school in Royalton, Wisconsin. She and Henry Conroy were engaged to marry. Henry worked as a laborer. They married on December 13, 1886. Before marrying, Mollie had saved most of her teacher's pay. She kept in contact with her siblings by writing them letters often. She knew about Ella attending a teacher training college and about her brother Richard living in Ripon, Wisconsin, 112 miles from the family home in Leon. Richard was studying to be a telegraphist. The training was difficult, but Richard was doing well. He was sending and receiving messages with increasing speed. Richard wrote to Mollie to ask for some money so that he could "have a little fun once in a while." He wrote, "It is fearful hard work to keep from going to dances or anything at all." He could not manage to have any spending money.

Letter writing was the means by which the now scattering Gogin siblings kept in touch about their own lives, as well as their parent's lives. Their father, Richard, had not learned to read nor write so he required the service of a neighbor to respond to letters written to him. The Gogin siblings kept aware of hometown news and news about the family farm. They knew about their mother Anna needing new teeth and that their father had a windmill installed on the farm. Ella wrote news about their aunts, those who lived in Wisconsin and those who lived in Philadelphia. Mollie was the confidante of her siblings. Her brother Richard wrote to her when he was in despair over losing a business he and a partner bought. Richard had saved money from his work at the railroad telegraph office. He and his partner bought a store. They planned to sell general merchandise. Shortly after the deal went through, Richard learned that his partner had taken their cash and absconded. He lost nearly everything. Richard had been hoping to demonstrate to his mother his business acumen. He wanted her to be proud of him. Mollie offered to send Richard some money but he declined her offer.

Gertrude Gogin was the next sister to begin a teaching career. She had dreams of going west. At nineteen years old, she was ready for an adventure. She accepted an offer to teach for two weeks in Langdon, North Dakota. While she was there, Gertrude met Joseph Boyd. Joseph was a widower with one son. Gertrude and Joseph decided to marry. They settled in Langdon in 1892 and remained there for the rest of their lives. In 1893, Gertrude gave birth to a son, Richard, named for her father. She and Joseph became very well known and socially prominent in Langdon. Joseph ran a successful mercantile business. Gertrude was elected the president of the Langdon Women's Club and the Langdon Civic Improvement League. She was a member of the Degree of Honor Society and the Lady Forester Circle.

Gertrude had filed a tree claim when she had first arrived in Langdon. The Timber Culture Act of 1873-1893 allowed persons to acquire an extra 160 acres of land as long as they planted at least 40 acres in trees. A percentage of the total number of trees had to survive at least thirteen years.

On April 29, 1909, a tornado swept through the town of Langdon. Before the tornado hit, torrential rain had been falling. People working away from their houses fared better than those at home. The tornado touched down south of the town. Then, the winds rose again and the tornado came down at the south end of the town. Another updraft allowed the tornado to jump. This time, two grain elevators and the Great Northern Water Tank were hit. Still moving, the destructive winds flattened houses and the Methodist Church. Eight mansions were leveled. In one of these mansions, Gertrude was at home with her son. She was killed instantly when timber beams struck her. Richard was injured but lived. Gertrude was thirty-nine years old.

Ella Gogin had been living with Gertrude and Joseph only a few years earlier. Ella had taken out a tree claim too. She did not marry, preferring to teach school in Langdon. She liked to take part in amateur theatricals. She received high praise for her acting skills. She left teaching in 1910 to work as a stenographer. She lived in Williston, North Dakota where she boarded with a family. Eventually, she moved to Los Angeles, California. She continued working as a stenographer, this time for an attorney. Ella passed away in Los Angeles on January 3, 1922.

Mabel Gogin, the youngest of the siblings, was sometimes called Katie. She did not enter the teaching profession like her sisters. Instead, when she was twenty-three years old, in 1901, Mabel took a job as a clerk in a local merchandise store. She worked until 9:30 every day. Even in poor weather, people came into the store. Often, there was a crowd inside the store, served by twelve clerks. Mabel got along well with her colleagues. She was glad to be earning money and getting on with her life. She missed her siblings who now mostly lived far away from home. Three of the siblings were in North Dakota. Mollie was living in Michigan with her family. Sometimes, her brother John and his wife drove from their home to visit his parents and Mabel. They brought their baby girl Gertrude with them. Mabel sometimes went out with a young man named Martin Killeen. Mabel liked Martin's company although she was, at times, irritated with Martin when he did not show up at dances. She did not speak to Martin until her anger cooled. They married in 1904 and had one son. Martin was a building contractor. He and Mabel moved to Berlin, Wisconsin, but she returned home to visit her parents when she could.

Anna Cook Gogin's daughters' lives mirrored her own in some ways. The mother and daughters shared a common faith and ancestry. They all valued family life and made time to stay connected with each other. They all worked hard at whatever they undertook. They all moved to new places and began again where nothing was familiar. There were significant differences in Anna's daughters' lives compared to their mother's as well. The daughters grew up in times very different to their mother's younger years. Anna had very little formal education. All of her daughters benefited from higher education. All of her daughters worked at paying jobs away from home. While the Gogin sisters contributed to the family's income, they also had their own money to spend or save, and they were in charge of their earnings. No matter where their life journeys took them, at the end of their days, most of Anna's daughters were laid to rest in the cemetery near their first home in Wisconsin, close to their mother, father and brothers. However far they had roamed, there was still no place like home.

WYOMING:

Jury Duty

Annie O'Connor Monaghan Carroll

The Wyoming Territory was created on July 25, 1868 from parts of the lands comprising the Dakota, Utah and Idaho Territories. The first Territorial government was inaugurated on May 19, 1869. Later that same year, the Wyoming Territorial Legislature passed the 1869 Suffrage Act granting women the right to vote. Territorial Governor John Campbell signed the Suffrage Act into law on December 10, 1869. No other territory or state in the United States allowed women to vote and hold public office. Soon after its passage, the Suffrage Act changed the lives of six women in the Territory. One of these women was Annie O'Connor Monaghan, an Irish immigrant who had only recently arrived in Albany County, Wyoming Territory.

Annie O'Connor Monaghan was born in Ireland in 1845. Her mother was Mary O'Connor. Annie, her mother and at least one brother, Charles, emigrated from Ireland. They made their way from the East Coast to the Wyoming Territory where they were among the early residents of Albany County. By the year 1868, Annie was married to a soldier stationed at Fort Sanders in the Territory. The soldiers and the fort, built in 1866, were there to protect people passing through on the Overland Trail. Annie's husband died during a cholera outbreak in February 1868. Two months later, Annie gave birth to a baby boy she named Francis. She and Francis had no income. So Annie accepted an offer of employment in the home of Dr. John Franz, a surgeon attached to the fort. She worked as a domestic servant for the doctor and his family. She was allowed to keep Francis with her in the Franz home. Annie worked in this home for a number of years.

On March 1, 1870, Judge John Howe was set to preside over a grand jury trial in Laramie, Wyoming Territory. Judge Howe and another judge, Judge John Kingman, both supported the Suffrage Act. Since the Suffrage Act made it legal for women to hold public offices, the judges understood the law to include jury duty. The Albany County Commissioners included women and men in a pool from which potential jurors would be called. The commissioners were not in favor of women serving on juries or women's suffrage. Some people speculated that the commissioners agreed to include women candidates in the pool because they hoped any woman who served would make a poor showing which would then help lead to a repeal of the Suffrage Act.

In order for a woman to have her name in the jury pool, she had to state that she would become a citizen, if she was not already naturalized. She had to be at least twenty-one years old, the legal voting age. She also had to be considered a woman of good character. On March 7, 1870, six women, two of them recent immigrants to the United States, and six men from the citizen pool were called to serve. It was the first time women sat on a jury in the Wyoming Territory and in the United States. Annie Monaghan was one of the women. The others were Eliza Stewart, Mary Macklemore, Amelia Hatcher, Jane Hilton and Sarah Pease. Initially, the women were reluctant to serve in light of the public scorn directed toward them. Judges Howe and Kingman convinced the women of the importance and necessity of their service.

Sarah Pease kept a detailed account of the proceedings of the grand jury hearing. The jurors heard details of a murder case. Sarah noted that "the women took their charge seriously, despite the ridicule and rancor that they faced." She noted that the women carefully studied the laws that they were asked to rule on and were not reluctant to correct the jury foreman, Mr. Frederick Laycock, when he misinterpreted the Territorial statutes. The jury voted to convict in this first case. The defense attorney, Melville C. Brown, moved that the conviction against his client should not be allowed to stand since the jury included women. Judge Howe overruled Brown's objection allowing the conviction to stand. Judge Howe stated that the women jurors conducted themselves admirably. He wrote an article for the *Chicago Legal News* describing the women's exemplary service.

The news about the case and the women jurors spread throughout the country. Particularly, for those championing the cause of women's suffrage in other parts of the country, the news gave them great hope. That hope was short-lived, however. After Judge Howe stopped presiding in October 1871, his replacement did not allow women to serve on juries. No explanation was given for the change. Even with the support of men formerly opposed to women sitting on juries, like the attorney Melville Brown, the prohibition against women serving on juries remained in Wyoming until 1949.

Annie Monaghan and the other women returned to their lives after their service as jurors. Annie met James Carroll, a stockman, in Laramie.

They married on October 30, 1870 in her mother's home. The family remained in Laramie for a few years but then moved to the Dakota Territory in 1875. In 1880, they lived in Centennial Prairie, Lawrence County, Dakota Territory with Annie's son Francis and four more children. In later years, Annie's mother came to live with her family.

The six women who served as the first female jurors in the Wyoming Territory are one reason that Wyoming today is known as the Equality State. Annie O'Connor Monaghan Carroll, once a young Irish immigrant, did realize her dream in America after many years of hard work. Those years of hard work may have contributed to her death at the age of fifty-seven years in 1902. Annie also did her part to help other women realize their dreams by serving as a role model in women's struggle for equality in the early years of Wyoming's Territorial and State history.

"First Woman's jury" Created by Ludwig & Stevenson Studio Photographs; 1940 copy of original photograph. Courtesy of American Heritage Center, University of Wyoming

Bibliography

"A Brief History of Our First One-Hundred Years!" The Wayback Machine https://web.archive.org/web/20100323011350/Hppy://www.asu.edu/~idmcs/mfc2a/history.html

Agricultural Census Maryland 1880

Alabama Women's Hall of Fame. "Margaret Murray Washington" www.awhf.org

Albany.com. "The City of Troy, New York-Centrally Located in the Capital Region." www.albany.com/neighborhoods/troy

American Battlefield Trust. "Albert Cashier aka Jennie Hodgers." www.battlefields.org

American Red Cross. "Red Cross National History." www.redcross.org

Ancestry. www.ancestry.com

Anderson, Andrea. *Rosalie Hart Priour and Annie Fagan Teal: Loyalty to the Land in the Irish Colonies of Mexican Texas.* https://scholarworks.calstate.edu

Archives Sisters of Charity. "Sister Mary de Sales." www.srcharitycinti.org/who-we-are/archives

Ashcroft, Mary Ann. "Woman Escaped Potato Famine, Sued B&O Railroad and Bought Eldersburg Farm." *Carroll Yesteryears*, May 13, 2018

Ashcroft, Mary Ann. "Yesteryears: An Irish immigrant woman in the 1800s took on the B&O Railroad and won." *Carroll County Times*, March 13, 2022. https://www.baltimoresun.com

Asheville Citizen-Times. "Mother Annie Colclough of St. Genevieve's Dies." December 1, 1942, pg. 8 www.newspapers.com/image/196235066

The Baltimore Sun. "The State of Maryland use of Hannah Dougherty." December 18, 1869, pg. 4.

The Baltimore Sun. "Proceedings of the Courts." December 22, 1869, pg. 4.

The Baltimore Sun. "Ten thousand Dollars Damages." October 4, 1870.

Bartlett, James. "Eva McGown: the never-forgotten Hostess of Fairbanks." *Fairbanks Daily News-Miner*, August 23, 2023.

Basilica of St. Joseph Porto-Cathedral https://stjosephbasilica.org/history

Bellamy, Jay. "Fireworks, Hoopskirts-and Death." Spring 2012, vol. 44, No. 1 www.archives.gov

Blanton, Deanne and Cook, Lauren. *They Fought Like Demons: Women Soldiers in the Civil War.* Baton Rouge, LA: Louisiana State Press, 2002.

Books, Moniek. "Abigail Campbell Kawananakoa-A prominent Princess." December 12, 2020 https://www.historyofroyalwomen.com

Boyd's Directory of the District of Columbia. Washington, D.C.1864 www.onlinebooks.library.upenn.edu

Bradsher, Greg, Dr. "Women Homesteaders." *National Archives,* September 2, 2012 https://text-message.blogs.archives.gov

Brown, Janice. "New Hampshire WWI Military: Army Nurse Corp's Teresa Margaret Murphy of Concord, NH (1891-1918) *Cow Hampshire Blog* www.cowhampshireblog.com

Bryson, Janice Ryan and Wood, Kathleen Shappee. *Irish Arizona.* Charleston, SC: Arcadia Publishing, 2008.

Buckman, Mary Jeremy, RSM. "Sister Mary Teresa Farrell." Mercy International Association https://www.mercyworld.org

Bucy, Carole Stanford."Biographical Sketch of Catherine Talty Kenny."
Alexander Street Part III. *Mainstream Suffragists-national American
Woman Suffrage Association* https://documents.alexanderstreet.com

Bucy, Carole Stanford. "Catherine Talty Kenny." Tennessee Historical
Society, October 8, 2017 http://tnency.utk.tennessee.edu

Butler, Nic Ph.D. "The Unmarked Grave of Ellen O'Donovan Rossa."
Charleston County Public Library https://www.ccph.org

BVM Foundress Mary Frances Clarke. "Mary Frances Clarke."
www.bvmsisters.org

Byrnes, Kim. "The Greening of Carroll County." *Carroll Magazine*
https://carrollmagazine.com/Carroll's-irish-roots

Carroll, Austin. "In the Wilds of Arkansas." *Leaves from
the Annals of the Sisters of Mercy.* Catholic Publication
Society. 327-372, 1881 Public Domain.

Carroll, Austin. "Starting Over." *Leaves from the Annals of the Sisters of
Mercy.* Catholic Publication Society. 129-142, 1881 Public Domain.

Causes, Carol Ann. "William Kehoe: Fulfilling the American
Dream." Savannah Biographies. 197 Georgia Southern
University, Digital Commons@Georgia Southern University
1991. https://digitalcommons.georgiasouthern.edu

Centers for Disease Control. "How TB Spreads." CDC Featured Snippets
www.cdc.gov

"Central City." www.unco.edu>mining-towns January 21, 2024.

Citizen Times. "Today in history: St. Genevieve-of-the-Pines school
opens." Asheville, NC January 6, 2016 www.citizen-times.com

City of Boise. "O'Farrell Family History." www.cityofboise.org

Clarke University. "About Mary Frances Clarke." www.clarke.edu

Clum, John P. "Nellie Cashman." *Arizona History Review* 3: 9-34, January 1931.

Cobb, Geoffrey. "Forgotten Legacies of Dr. Gertrude Kelly." *New York Irish History* Vol.32 2018 https://nyirishhistory.us

Collar Laundry Union. "Kate Mullany-Collar Laundry Union 1864-Troy, New York." https://libcom.org/

College History Garden. "Remembering St. Genevieve-of-the-Pines college in Asheville, NC." *Citizen Times.* January 22, 2017 https://collegehistorygarden.blogspot.com/2017/01

"Colorado Milling and Elevator Co. http://denvercolor.com January 20,2024.

Coming, Alison. "Clogherhead hero recalled in new book on Irish in America." *Irish Independent* November 16, 2021.

Commins, Pat and Rice, Elizabeth. *Irish Immigrants in Michigan: A History in Stories.* Charleston, SC: The History Press, 2021.

Convery, William J. III. *Pride of the Rockies: The Life of Colorado's Premiere Irish Patron, John Kernan Mullen.* Boulder, CO 2000: 35-39.

CSJ St. Paul Archive. "O'Connor, Sister Anita-1865-1956." https://csjstpaularchives.catalogaccess.com/archives/2632

"Daytona State College Renames College of Workforce and Continuing Education in Honor of Mary Brennan Karl." January 27, 2020. www.daytonastate.edu

"Death of a Maine Philanthropist." *Boston Globe,* Monday, November 5, 1883.

Dickinson, Emily. "I'm Nobody! Who are you?" In The Poems of Emily Dickinson: Variorum Edition, edited by Ralph W. Franklin. Cambridge, MA: The Belknap Press of Harvard University Press, 1998.

Dreilinger, Danielle. "Home Work: Mass incarceration and Margaret Murray Washington." Dec 16, 2020 https://did.substack.com

Edson, Leah Jackson. "Biographies of Edward and Teresa Eldridge." *The Fourth Corner*, 1968, pg.28 https://www.stumpranchonline.com/skagitjournal

Elliot, Sally. "Jennie Judge Kearns: My Story." Park City Historical Society. & Museum https://parkcityhistory.org

Elliot, Sally. "John Judge: My Story." Park City Historical Society & Museum https://parkcityhistory.org

Elliot, Sally. "Thomas Kearns: My Story." Park City Historical Society & Museum https://parkcityhistory.org

Emily Dickinson Museum. "Emily Dickinson and Death." www.emilydickinsonmuseum.org

Encyclopedia of Cleveland History. "Ignatia, Sister Mary, CSA." https://case.edu

Espiritu, Allison. "Margaret Murray Washington (1865-1925) February 15, 2007 BlackPast.org

Find A Grave. www.findagrave.com

Florida Women's Hall of Fame. www.flwomenshalloffame.org

Ford, Martin. "The Irish Girl and the American Letter: Irish Immigrants in 19th Century America." *The Irish Story* November 17, 2018 www.theirishstory.com

Gardner, Elizabeth. "Sister Mary Ignatia helped pioneer treatment, care for alcoholics." www.modernhealthcare.com

Geisen, David. "Kate Kennedy: Historical Essay." www.foundsf.org

Genealogical and Historical Research Service in Ireland. "County Louth: Jennie Hodgers." www.mc-research.com/county-louth

Gillespie, Tom. "Alcoholics Anonymous co-founder had Mayo roots." www.con-telegraph.ie/2021/01/09

Gleeson, David. "Irish." *South Carolina Encyclopedia*. June 8, 2016 https://www.scencyclopedia.org

Gorn, Elliot J. "The History of Mother Jones". *Mother Jones Magazine* May/June 2001 www.motherjones.com

Graham, Harold. "The First Wave of Irish Immigrants to Beat 3 Newton County, Mississippi." www.nchgs.org

"Hannah Curtis, writing from Queens County, Ireland to her brother John Curtis in Philadelphia." Re-imagining Migration https://reimaginingmigration.org

Hartzog, Sister Grace, SC. "Sisters of Charity of St. Joseph's and slavery." Sisters of Charity Federation, February 9, 2022 https://sistersofcharityfederation.org

Historical Society of Pennsylvania. "Curtis Family." https://hsp.org

Historical Society of Pennsylvania. "Irish Immigrant Letters Home." https://hsp.org

History Link. "The donation Land claim Act." https://www.historylink.org/file/9501

Homestead Act (1862) National Archives
https://www.archives.gov/milestone-documents/homestead-act

Holmes, David G. *The Letters of the Gogin Family, 1877-1908: Irish in Wisconsin.* Madison, WI: Wisconsin Historical Society Press, 2004. E-book edition 2013 pgs. 60-87.

Huddersfield Local History Society. "Huddersfield History." www.huddersfieldhistory.org.uk

Hume, Larry E. Chief Master Sergeant, U.S. Airforce, Retired. "Teresa Margaret Murphy." www.findagrave.com/memorial/56503711

Hunter, Robert. "Mary Karl key figure in DBCC history." *Daytona Beach News-Journal.* December 7, 1997.

Idaho Daily Statesman. "Funeral to Be Held Thursday." Boise, Idaho www.newspapers.com/image/722051647

Irishacw. "Hard Graft & Grasshopper: Irish Homesteaders in 1870s Nebraska." December 3, 2016. https://irishamericancivilwar.com/2016/12/03

Isabelle Ahearn O'Neill Papers. Rhode Island Historical Society, Manuscripts Division https://www.rihs.org

"J.K. Mullen, Catholic Benefactor, Carved Empire Out of Colorado Wilderness." *The Denver Catholic Register.* July 10, 1952 www.archives.archden.org

Jordan, Donals & O'Keefe, Timothy J. *The Irish Literary and Historical Society of the San Francisco Bay Area.* San Francisco, CA 2005. www.ilhssf.org

Karst, James. "Margaret Haughery: Friend of orphans-and of white supremacist militia." *The Times-Picayune*, July 12, 2019 www.nola.com.

Kazan, Michael. "Irish Families in Portland, Oregon, 1850-1880, an immigrant culture in the Far West." (1974) dissertations and Theses. Paper 2230 https://pdxscholar.library.pdx.edu

Kemp, David. *The Irish in Dakota*. Sioux Falls, SD: Rushmore House Publishing, 1992, pg. 116.

King, Roxanne. "J.K. Mullen's 'legendary' Catholic philanthropy endures in Colorado today." December 1, 2022 https://denvercatholic.org

Kingsbury, George W. *History of Dakota Territory*. Chicago, IL: S.J. Clarke Publishing Company, 1915, pgs. 690-698.

League of Women Voters. "How Native American Women Inspired the Women's Suffrage Movement." November 29, 2021 www.lwv.org

"Leaving the Emerald Isle". Irish Immigration to Philadelphia. http://hsp.org

Legends of Tuskegee: "Booker T. Washington Personal Life." https://www.nps.gov/museum/exhibits/tuskegee/btwlife.htm

Lemons, J. Stanley. "Biographical Sketch of Isabelle Ahearn O'Neill." Included in Part III, *Mainstream Suffragists-National American Woman Suffrage Association*. documents.alexanderstreet.com

Library of Virginia. "Pauline Forstall Colclough Adams Wrote To Her Son From Prison." October 23, 1917 https://edu.lva.virginia.gov

Lindenmeyer, Kriste. *Ordinary Women, Extraordinary Lives: Women in American History*. Wilmington, DE: Scholarly Resources Inc. 2000, pgs. 197-213.

Lindgren, H. Elaine. *Land in Her Own Name*. North Dakota Institute for Regional Studies. Fargo, ND: North Dakota State University, 1991 pgs. 200-210, 264.

Lucky, William L., S.J. "Two Irish Merchants of New England."
New England Quarterly. Vol., XIV, Number 4, December 1941.

Maine: An Encyclopedia. "Kavanagh, Edward."
www.maineencyclopedia.com/edward-kavanagh

"Margaret Maher's Amherst". https://archive.emilydickinson.org

Masson, Thomas. "Red Cross Nurses." Poetryparc.
wordpress.com www.poemhunter.com

McCarron, Edward Thomas. "The world of Kavanagh and control:
A portrait of Irish emigration, entrepreneurship, and ethnic diversity
in mid-Maine, 1760-1820." Durham, NH: University of New
Hampshire, 1992. https://scholars.unh.edu/dissertation/1683

McCormack, Eileen R. "Hill, Mary Theresa Mehegan (1846-1921)."
Mnopedia, September 2, 2015. Modified December 7, 2017.
www.mnopedia.org

McCormick, S. San Francisco, California Directory.
"Anne Fitzpatrick Armstrong." Accessed through www.ancestry.com 1868.

McCormick, S. Portland, Oregon City Directory 1822-1995. "Anne
Fitzpatrick Armstrong." Accessed through www.ancestry.com 1884, 1888.

McNally, Frank. "A Miner with a heart of gold-An Irishman's Diary
about the extraordinary Nellie Cashman. *Irish Times*, April 28, 2017.

Mercies, Laurie K. "We Are Women Irish: Gender, Class, Religious,
and Ethnic Identity in Anaconda, Montana." *Montana the magazine
of Western History*, Winter, Vol. 44, No. 1 pgs. 28-41. Montana
Historical Society 1994. http://www.jstor.com/stable/4519649

Meyerriecks, Maryanne. "Fort Smith finds out about Mother
Mary Teresa Farrell." *Arkansas Catholic*. October 31, 2019.

Minnesota Historical Society. "Mary Theresa Hill." www.mnhs.org/hillhouse

"Miss Winifred Kavanagh." *Boston Evening Transcript*, Thursday, September 27, 1883, pg. 4.

Molly Brown House Museum. "A Devoted and Inspirational Mother." https://mollybrown.org

Montana Standard Butte. "Mrs. Armstrong Succumbs At 86." January 31, 1936 pg. 5 www.newspapers.com

Moore, Charles. *History of Michigan*. V.2. Chicago, IL: The Lewis Publishing Company, 1915. 986-987.

Mother Jones Museum. "Mother Jones." www.motherjonesmuseum.org

Mount Callaghan(NV) climbing, Hiking & Mountaineering: Summit Post. "History of Dan Callaghan." www.summitpost.org/mount-Callaghan-no/773425

Mullen, Kevin. "James Campbell: Bishop Street boy who married Hawaiian royalty and shaped Oahu." *Derry Journal*, July 8, 2022.

Mulrooney, Margaret M. *Black Powder White Lace: the du Pont Irish and Cultural Identity in Nineteenth-Century America*. Lebanon, NH: University Press, 2002.

Multnomah County Marriages. "Anne Fitzpatrick Armstrong." https://gfo.org/resources/indexes/ital-records/multnomah-county-marriage

Murphy, Pauline. "The remarkable tale of a Louth woman who fought in the American Civil War." *Irish Central* March 27, 2017 www.irishcentral.com/roots

National Park Service. "Early Choctaw History-Natchez Trace Parkway." www.nps.gov

"Nellie Cashman (1844-1925)." AWHF https://www.azwhf.org

Nevada Women's History Project. "Jessie Callahan Mahoney."
https://nevadawomen.org

Newspapers.com. "First Service Flag Flown For New Hampshire Women."
www.newspapers.com/image/56547533

Newspapers.com. "Funeral Services Are Held For Pioneer."
Reno Evening Gazette, Thursday, October 19, 1933, pg. 6.

New Mexico Historic Women. "Sisters of Charity-New Mexico
Historic Women Marker Program." www.nmhistoricwomen.org

New York Celtic Medical Society. "Gertrude B. Kelly."
www.celticmedsocnyc.org/gertrude-b-Kelly

Nicholson, Joyce Willis. NCHGS Willis Family-Newton
County Historical & Genealogical Society www.nchgs.org

Nineteenth Amendment to the U.S. Constitution: Women's Right to
Vote https://www.archives.gov/milestone-documents/19th-amendment

North Carolina, U.S., Naturalization Records, 1872-1996.
"Annie Mary Josephine Colclough." January 22, 1925
www.ancestry.com/discoveryui-content/view/276184:2503

North Dakota, U.S. Naturalizations, 1873-1952. "Maggie
O'Connor." www.ancestry.com/imageviewwe/collections/62035

O'Brien, Michael I. "Irish Pioneers in Kentucky: Irish Catholic
Settlements." New York, NY: *The Gaelic American*, 1916.

O'Neill, Aliyah. "How an Irish maid saved Emily Dickinson's
poetry." *Irish Central*, June 20, 2023 www.irishcentral.com

Parker, Robert Dale. *The Sound the Stars Make Rushing
Through the Sky: The Writings of Jane Johnston Schoolcraft.*
Philadelphia, PA: University of Pennsylvania Press, 2007.

"Pauline Adams". Virginia Changemakers https://edu.lva.virginia.gov

Pauline Forstall Colclough Adams, Papers, 1917-1990. Accession 37402, Personal Papers Collections, Library of Virginia, Richmond, Virginia

"Pauline Forstall Colclough Adams (1874-1957). Turning Point Suffragist Memorial https://suffragistmemorial.org

Pawlak, Patricia. "The Diary of Mary McKeon, an Irish American Domestic Servant in Nineteenth Century America." August 31, 2016. https://hdl.handle.net/10161/12714

Payne, Joshua. "The Billy the Kid Connection: Catherine McCarty and the Beginnings of Wichita." www.sedgwickcounty.org

Poetry Foundation. "Emily Dickinson." www.poetryfoundation.org/poets/emily-dickinson

Portland Daily Press. "Death of Miss Winifred Kavanagh." Portland, Maine, November 5, 1883, pg. 1.

Reno Gazette-Journal. "Fell From His Wagon." Friday, August 13, 1886, pg. 3.

Rex, Joyce A. Purcell, Register. "Erin Springs." December 22, 1983 https://okgenweb.net

Rhode Island Heritage Hall of Fame. "Isabelle Florence Ahearn O'Neill." https://riheritagehalloffame.com

Rhode Island Historical Society. "Isabelle Ahearn O'Neill." https://rihs.minisisinc.com

Rossa, Jeremiah O'Donovan. *Rossa's recollections, 1838 to 1898*. Mariners Harbor, NY: 1898.

Roth, Charlotte Roeder. "Profiles and Obituaries of the Eldridge Family: Edward and Teresa Eldridge." History of Whatcom County, 1926 www.stumpranchonline.com/skagitjournal

Ryniker, Sarah. "Savannah's Ethnic Irish Neighborhoods in the Nineteenth Century: A Historical Multimethod Examination." Georgia Southern University 2017. https://digitalcommons.georgiasouthern.edu

Saldana, Brittny and Kendrick, Jen. "Colorado Irish Immigrants." https://mollybrown.org/Irish-diaspora-and-colorado

Sanders, Helen Fitzgerald. *A History of Montana*. Chicago, IL: Lewis Publishing Company 1913, pg. 886.

Schoolcraft, Henry. *The Literary Voyager* or *Muzzeniegun*. Edited by Mason, Philip P. East Lansing, MI: Michigan State University Press, 1962.

Sessions, Gene. "Years of Struggle: the Irish in the Village of Northfield, 1845-1900." www.vermonthistory.org. Vol. 55, No. 2 Spring 1997

Shaw, Luella. *True History of some of the Pioneers of Colorado*. Hotchkiss, CO: W.S. Coburn, 1909.

Simonson, Pauline. "Kearns-St. Ann's Orphanage." Utah Historical Markers www.utahhistoricalmarkers.org

Sisters of St. Joseph of Carondelet and Consociates St. Paul Province. *Archive* https://csjstpaul.org/community/history/archive

Sisters of Charity. "S. Mary De Sales Leheny." www.srcharitycinti.org/2019/04/04

Smith, George Martin. *South Dakota: its History and Its People*. Chicago, IL: S.J. Clarke Publishing Company, 1915.

Snodgrass, Mary Ellen. *Settlers of the American West*. Jefferson, NC: McFarland & Company, Inc. 2015. 123-124.

Terrell, Ellen. "An almost inexcusable catastrophe-explosion at the Washington Arsenal." Library of Congress blogs, June 19, 2015 https://blogs.loc.gov

"Ten Lives the Toll Of Tornadoes". *The Evening Times*, Grand Forks, North Dakota, Monday, May 31, 1909 https://tile.loc.gov

The American Federation of Labor and congress of Industrial Organizations. "Mother Jones." www.AFL-CIO.org

The Antrim Family. "Catherine McCarty-Antrim." www.aboutbillythekid.com

The Daytona Daily News. Daytona Beach, Florida January 2, 1921.

The Daytona Daily News. Daytona Beach, Florida February 6, 1921.

The Dupont Company on the Brandywine. "Immigration 1803-1855. www.hagley.org

The Dupont Company on the Brandywine. "Ports of Arrival and Departure." www.hagley.org

The Dupont Company on the Brandywine. "The Passage: Life at Sea." www.hagley.org

The Dupont Company on the Brandywine. "The People." www.hagley.org

"The Explosion Yesterday at the Arsenal". *Evening Star*. Washington, District of Columbia, June 18, 1864, pg. 1 www.newspapers.com

"The Funeral of the Victims of the Arsenal Explosion". *Evening Star*. Washington, District of Columbia, June 20, 1864, pg. 1 www.newspapers.com

"The ladies of the Laramie jury; First in the world to serve-1870." Albany County Historical Society (ACHS) www.wyoachs.com

"The Midleton Woman who became a Queen in America." Ring of Cork. https://www.ringofcork.ie

The O'Leary/Hart family's years in Texas. www.stmichaelsblackrock.ie

"The Panama Route". UC Press E-Books Collection, pgs. 252-253 https://publishing.cdlib.org

The Sisters of Charity of St. Augustine. "Sister Ignatia Gavin" www.sisters@srsofcharity.org

The State Historical Society of North Dakota. "Acquiring the Land: The Land Shaped by Lincoln: Lincoln's Legacy Online Exhibit." www.history.nd.gov

The Times. "Mary Karl." Harbor Beach, Michigan August 6, 1948.

"The Trail of Tears: Why we remember." www.choctawnation.com

Thompson, Taylor. "Biographical Sketch of Pauline Adams/Alexander Street Documents" https://documents.alexanderstreet.com

Today in History-December 10 Library of Congress www.loc.gov

Traynor, Jessica. "The Life of the Irishwoman who was inducted into the Alabama Women's Hall of Fame. *Irish Times*, December 18, 2019.

"Tribute Is Paid To Pioneer Woman." *Bellingham Herald*, Bellingham, Washington, Friday, May 12, 1911, pg. 1 www.newspapers.com

University of Alaska. "Eva McGown: UAF Rehearsal Hall Bears Name of Fairbanks Hostess." https://www.alaska.edu

University of New Mexico. "Leheny, Sister Mary de Sales." 1976-ongoing, box: 1 Folder 58. UNM Center for Southwest Research & Special Collections https://nmarchives.unm.edu

University of Wyoming American Heritage Center photos Re-enactment of first women jurors created 1880s www.uwyo.edu

Viner, Kim. "Women on the Jury: Wyoming Makes History Again." www.wyohistory.org

Walworth, Dorothy. "The Love of Eva McGown." *Reader's Digest* 58: 349, May 1951.

Webb, Benjamin J. *The Centenary of Catholicity in Kentucky: Bardstown Settlement.* Louisville, KY: Charles A. Rogers, 1884.

West Virginia Encyclopedia. "Mother Jones." www.wvencyclopedia.org

"Whatcom County Established in 1854" www.whatcomcounty.us

Wright, Mary C. "The World of Women: Portland, Oregon, 1860-1880." (1973) Dissertations and Theses. Paper 1990 Portland State University https://pdxscholar.library.pdx.edu

Women & the American Story. "Life Story: Margaret Haughery." https://was.nyhistory.org

Women History Blog. "Jane Johnston Schoolcraft." www.womenhistoryblog.com/2012/07/jane-Johnston-Schoolcraft

Women Homesteaders-Homestead National Historical Park Nebraska www.nps.gov

Wyoming History www.wyo.gov

Young, Patrick, Esq. "The Washington Arsenal Explosion: Irish Women and Girls Killed Recklessly." July 31, 2016 https://longislandwins.com

About The Authors

Pat Commins was born in Ardee, County Louth, Ireland. He is a retired teacher and administrator who studied at St. Mary's College, Strawberry Hill, Twickenham, London and University College Dublin. Pat has traveled widely throughout his career. He is a student of Irish history, which he has shared through many presentations in Ireland and the United States. Pat lives in Dublin, Ireland.

Elizabeth Rice is a retired teacher who lives in Michigan. Elizabeth graduated with a Bachelor of Arts degree from Albion College. She earned a Master of Arts in Education from the University of Michigan. Elizabeth has a keen interest in people and their stories. Along with Pat Commins, Elizabeth has shared many presentations on Irish history and Michigan history, as told through the life stories of people.

www.ingramcontent.com/pod-product-compliance
Lightning Source LLC
Chambersburg PA
CBHW051147120626
46547CB00012B/978